i will
scream
to the
world

i will scream to the world

JAHA MARIE DUKUREH

Foreword by
ASHLEY JUDD

KENSINGTON PUBLISHING CORP.
www.kensingtonbooks.com

CONTENT WARNINGS: Physical Abuse, Sexual Abuse, Verbal Abuse, Parental Death, Terminal Illness, Sexism/Misogyny, Sexual Assault

DAFINA BOOKS are published by

Kensington Publishing Corp.
900 Third Ave.
New York, NY 10022

All Kensington Titles, Imprints, and Distributed Lines are available at special quantity discounts for bulk purchases for sales promotions, premiums, fund-raising, and educational or institutional use. Special book excerpts or customized printings can also be created to fit specific needs. For details, write or phone the office of the Kensington special sales manager: Kensington Publishing Corp., 900 Third Ave., New York, NY 10022, Attn: Special Sales Department, Phone: 1-800-221-2647.

Library of Congress Control Number: 2024943021

The DAFINA logo is a trademark of Kensington Publishing Corp.

ISBN: 978-1-4967-4846-1
First Kensington Hardcover Edition: January 2025

ISBN: 978-1-4967-4848-5 (ebook)

10 9 8 7 6 5 4 3 2 1

Printed in the United States of America

*This book is dedicated to
the women and girls of the world.
May they suffer no more.
May they thrive and achieve their dreams.*

Contents

Dedication • v

Foreword • ix

Introduction • 1

PART 1: SURVIVOR • 5

CHAPTER 1: The Child Bride • 7

CHAPTER 2: The Gambian Girl • 16

CHAPTER 3: Coming to America • 28

CHAPTER 4: The Immigrant Girl • 34

CHAPTER 5: My Mum, My Dad • 39

CHAPTER 6: Losing Hope • 51

CHAPTER 7: Surrender and Perseverance • 58

PART 2: ACTIVIST • 65

CHAPTER 8: A Daughter Inspires • 67

CHAPTER 9: The Underground Activist • 73

CHAPTER 10: Going Public • 82

CHAPTER 11: Safe Hands for Girls • 90

CHAPTER 12: Unexpected Victories • 102

CHAPTER 13: Becoming a "Hero" • 112

CHAPTER 14: The Making of *Jaha's Promise* • 118

CHAPTER 15: Social Activism Meets Beauty • 122

CHAPTER 16: The Fight Continues • 129

CHAPTER 17: Developing Young Leaders • 136

CHAPTER 18: It Takes a Village • 143

PART 3: HUMAN • 151

CHAPTER 19: Love Found and Lost • 153

CHAPTER 20: Becoming a Whole Woman • 171

CHAPTER 21: A Focus on Mental Health • 176

CHAPTER 22: Children as Hope • 180

CHAPTER 23: Africa, My Africa • 185

CHAPTER 24: Madam President? • 193

CHAPTER 25: Final Reflections • 213

Notes • 225

FGM Resources • 227

Child Marriage Resources • 234

Economic Empowerment/Development Resources • 240

Acknowledgments • 249

Epilogue • 251

Foreword

FEMALE GENITAL MUTILATION (FGM) first came to my awareness when I started my international humanitarian work in 2002. I began to sit with girls who had been subjected to the rite, with mothers, aunties, and the men who insisted on the practice as a condition for marriage, and even with the cutters of genitals themselves. I learned about the cultural roots of FGM and the justifications for its practice, primary among them the need to control women's insatiable sexuality and to ensure virginity before marriage, fidelity after. This both galled me and did not surprise me. Men's fear and hatred of the female body—our sexuality—are pervasive in societies around the world, including the United States, as is the desire to control it. FGM is the literal physical expression of this pathological control.

In 2014 I heard about an online petition to abolish FGM, posted by Jaha Dukureh, a twenty-four-year-old Gambian mother then living in Atlanta. Having been brutalized by FGM as an infant, Jaha was married off at the age of fifteen to a much older man, who abused her and whom she was eventually able to divorce. After giving birth to a daughter by her second husband, she became determined not to allow FGM happen to her child or to any other girl. At great personal risk, she became the face behind the movement to eliminate FGM. As a consequence, many in her family and community ostracized her, she was upbraided for bringing shame to her heritage and her religion, and she began to receive threats to her life. But she refused to back down, despite the high cost she had to pay.

I figured that if Jaha had the courage to wage this battle after everything she had been through, the least I could do was sign her petition and encourage my followers on social media to join me. Eventually, the petition gained nearly a quarter of a million signatures, which led to President Obama commissioning a report that captured the shocking prevalence of FGM even in our own country, despite the fact that FGM is illegal here. Thanks to Jaha, the invisible was made visible, and there are now programs to educate people about the serious physical and psychological damage done by cutting.

But Jaha's successes go far beyond that. She helped create legal change in the Gambia, where the president banned FGM in 2015, an astonishing turnabout in a country where virtually every girl was subjected to FGM. She has received multiple honors, including being one of the youngest Africans to be nominated for a Nobel Peace Prize, becoming a UN Goodwill Ambassador, and being recognized as one of Time 100's most influential people. When she was only twenty-eight, Jaha was the subject of a documentary chronicling her fight to end FGM. And in 2021 she even became a candidate for president of the Gambia.

Jaha's story moves me deeply. She and I come from vastly different cultures and backgrounds, yet we are bound by a remarkable number of similarities. We have both had tumultuous family lives. We have both lost our beloved mothers. We have both walked with mental and physical health challenges. We are both survivors of male sexual assault. We are also both public figures, which has empowered us in our fight for change but also left us vulnerable to extraordinary amounts of online abuse and hatred.

Yet we have both remained committed to social justice. We fight against sex- and gender-based violence. We believe that education and financial independence are crucial steps for freeing women from misogyny and male violence. We are outspoken. We tell our personal stories honestly and without reservation. Which is why I feel it is not just a duty but also a sacred honor to support Jaha in her indefatigable efforts to spare girls and women the bodily harm and psychological trauma that she endured.

As you read this wonderful book Jaha has written, I hope she gives you the courage to tell your own story. A scream from the heart can split a soul wide open. Our world needs to see, hear, feel, and know women's souls.

Remember, your voice is your power. The power of story. The power of struggle. The power of fragility. The power of persistence. The power of love for those in need of allies who are willing to take their own risks to support their protection.

So, use it well, just as Jaha has done.

—Ashley Judd, Actor, Activist,
and *New York Times* bestselling Author

i will
scream
to the
world

Introduction

"As long as I am alive, I will wake up every single day and scream to the world that FGM is wrong and child marriage is not different from rape."

—*Jaha Marie Dukureh*

WORDS HAVE POWER, AND WHEN you are a public figure, your words become amplified. They live on after a media interview or event and have a no-expiration shelf life on the Internet. They come to define you and become part of your legacy.

I Will Scream to the World came deeply from my heart after years of working as an activist. I believe most changemakers scream to the world, no matter what their cause. The pain of loss from an environmental catastrophe. Another ethnic genocide. The massacre of innocents during war. Devastation from disease because of racism and poverty. The screaming comes not just from the big horrors. Oftentimes, the most shattering moments are intensely personal. Holding the hand of a woman who has been raped, carrying a child weak from starvation, watching a grown man sob because his family has been slaughtered.

We are not and cannot be silent. We are screamers.

Yet my face to the public has never been that of a woman who is screaming. An important reason for my effectiveness as an activist is I listen hard and speak softly. I am the exact opposite of a screamer, because I know the war against the abuse of women will not be won with shrillness and tirades. Female genital mutilation (FGM) will not end because of violent rhetoric. Young girls will not escape the horrors of being child brides through raised voices.

1

Instead, I quietly debate. I give facts and share stories. I plant seeds and nourish ideas. I am cautious with both my voice and my body language. I publicly show little emotion when confronted with personal attacks and threats. I never break down in front of people. Rather, I act like I am not bothered by hateful words and actions.

As a survivor of FGM and two child marriages, and as a witness to the unbearable pain of thousands of young girls and women, I will tell you I scream inside every day. What has been done to me and what I have seen cause me sleepless nights and anguished tears in private. The physical, emotional, and spiritual pain does not go away.

For most of my life, I have buried my screams very deeply. I knew I could not accomplish what I needed if I let those screams overwhelm me. I could not do what I have been placed here on earth to do—to ease the suffering of millions of women. I have paid a heavy price for my outward calm. For such a long time, I was not whole. I never allowed myself to heal. I went from victim to survivor to activist, but I did not take the next step of acknowledging that I was human, after all. I did not let myself thrive personally.

While so many called me a "hero," I still felt broken. That trope of the broken hero is so much a part of our world. Fictionally, it has given us such characters as Tony Stark, who morphs into Iron Man. We gravitate to "fallen" politicians and movie stars who find redemption. We delve deep into the lives of current and historical figures to determine what makes or made them tick.

However, behind every survivor turned activist and every victim turned hero is a human being just like you. We may look strong on the outside, but there are scars on the inside that can close off our hearts, so they feel like they cease to beat or smother our lungs, so every breath taken is difficult.

This book is about my journey from victim to survivor to activist. I was thirty-three years old when I wrote it, so it captures just three decades of my life and reflects how I saw life at this point. It is a compilation of who I was in the past, who I was at that moment in time, and who I hoped to become in the future.

I Will Scream to the World concerns the issues I have given my life to as a women's rights activist and a human rights activist: FGM, child marriage, poverty, racism, the lack of access to education, and more. Most importantly, it is about me becoming and being seen as a human, with the flaws, emotions, and dreams we all have.

To quote the great South African human rights activist Desmond Tutu: "My humanity is bound up in yours, for we can only be human together."

Those are powerful words. Now I share my own words with you.

SURVIVOR

I often ask myself, "Have I truly survived?" To me, the word survivor *feels inadequate, almost superficial, to describe the profound complexities of my experiences. It is because being a survivor is not about the destination or an endpoint. It is an ongoing expedition, a continuous dance of facing challenges, embracing vulnerabilities, and striving for equilibrium. To label myself as a "survivor" would be to ignore the ebbs and flows, the progress and regressions, and the intricate layers of healing and rediscovery that shape my identity.*

Some might say, "But you've made it through. You are here, aren't you? Is that not survival?" Indeed, by that logic, I have survived. But is survival merely the act of existing? Is it simply drawing breath and moving through days? Or is it an ever-evolving state of being that acknowledges the scars that pain leaves behind?

Chapter 1

The Child Bride

I CANNOT LOOK MY HUSBAND in the eye as I lie naked on our marriage bed. He has waited for seven years to take the young girl who was promised to him by my parents when I was only eight years old. I am fifteen now, and he is decades older than me. While I am unsure of his exact age, I am clear that what is happening to me is wrong. He presses into my untouched place but is not able to consummate our marriage, because my vagina is sewn shut.

It is a surprise for both of us. I was an infant when I was subjected to female genital mutilation (FGM). Not only were my clitoris and labia removed, but I was also sewn up. It is a common practice in my country, the Gambia. Seventy-six percent of women have been cut. But we are not unique. The World Health Organization estimates that more than two hundred million girls and women alive today have undergone FGM, which is also commonly referred to as cutting or circumcision.[1] That is equal to two-thirds of the population of the United States.

The irony is that in 2005, as I lie shaking underneath my husband, FGM prevents my husband from penetrating me. Oh, the people around me do not see this act in the same way I do. Not my dad. Not my family. Not my community. And certainly not the man who believes it is his absolute right to take a young girl as a wife against her will. After all, I am his prized child bride. Like FGM, my story is not unusual. Every year, for cultural, religious, and economic reasons, at least twelve million girls are married before they reach the age of eighteen.[2] This amounts to twenty-eight girls every minute.

Yet these numbers mean little to me as I lie in that cursed bed. It will be several years—when my daughter is born—before I see this atrocity as one that goes beyond my own personal hell. Quite simply, the number of children suffering just like me is too big for a naive young girl to grasp.

Only one number stands out in my mind while I grit my teeth against the pain flowing through my body and heart as my frustrated and furious husband stalks out of his bedroom. The number is fourteen. That is how old I was when my dad happily sent me to New York City to marry this man. There was no negotiation, no pleading, no listening to what I wanted and needed. There was absolutely no choice.

I left Africa for the United States in March 2005, grieving for my lost childhood and my mum, who had died six months earlier from breast cancer. When she was diagnosed, I had just entered middle school at one of the best private academic institutions in the Gambia. My activities were typical for a young teenager—studying, socializing with friends, and even having my first crush on a boy. My future husband was not often in my thoughts, except when kids would bully me if they found out I was already promised in marriage.

Most of my fellow classmates came from wealthy and powerful Gambian families. I was an anomaly in their world—an upper-class young girl from a very traditional tribe, whose father was an Imam, an Islamic religious leader. When I was growing up, my dad had three wives and more than thirty kids. There were so many, I could not even name my youngest siblings. Instead, I found myself asking, "Who's your mom?" Life in a large polygamous household was filled with drama and sometimes verbal, emotional, and physical abuse. My curious, outgoing, and adventuresome personality was visible only at school; at home, it was more about flight or fight.

At the core of the drama was my dad and mum's relationship.

His latest wife did not get along with my mum, and their arguments were often heated. By nature, my mum was a fighter. One day she had had enough of the insults and physically attacked her co-wife, who ran into another room. My mum started banging on the locked door, the door opened, and then I saw them get into a skirmish. My father got involved, and my mum got hurt. Blood started gushing out as she fell to the floor. None of the adults there lifted a finger to help her, leaving my older sister to find neighbors who could get my mum to the hospital.

I honestly cannot remember what I was doing when this was happening. Like with many memories from my youth, I have forgotten the details of my involvement, because this was necessary for my mental and emotional survival. Looking back, I realize I probably was stunned into inaction and stood powerless on the sidelines. In my world, women had little power to defend themselves against violence, and young girls even less. I believe any intervention on my part would have resulted in me lying on the floor, bleeding, like my mum. What I understand now is that day was the beginning of the end of my life as I knew it.

While my mother was being treated for her head wound, the doctors discovered she had breast cancer. She blamed my dad because she was convinced the blood from the injury had somehow traveled to her breast, causing the tumor. As a young girl, I believed her accusation. It made me resent my dad and his wife for what they had done to her. My mum told everyone how my dad had caused her to contract this disease. The news spread throughout our community, and I hated it. I did not want anyone to know what was happening at our house, because it mortified me.

During her treatment, one of her breasts was removed, and she became very self-conscious, especially when my stepmother made fun of her. Yet losing her breast did not stop the cancer from spreading. I do not think they were doing radiation therapy and chemotherapy in the Gambia back then. The doctors recommended she travel to the United Kingdom for more treatment. When she returned home, she seemed healthier and happier. She believed she was cured. I felt such joy.

But her fight was not over. The doctors determined she needed a second round of treatment in London. This time, she arranged for me to accompany her. I was excited since many of my fellow classmates traveled to the West on vacation. Even though my mum never told me directly why she pulled me out of school for the trip, I knew her primary reason was to give me something I had always dreamed about—the opportunity to see something of the world outside of the Gambia. On my first flight ever, I got my period and experienced terrible cramps. Between that and the turbulence, the plane ride left me terrified. I remember gripping the seat so tightly that my hands ached. It was all worth it when we arrived in London. People of so many nationalities surrounded me, and I saw that women there were treated very differently than women were in my country.

But this was not a pleasure trip: I was there to help my mum. The chemo was tough on her. We went shopping and sightseeing on good days, but those outings were few and far between. She was a very strong woman and did everything she could not to show how much she was suffering. She always kept her smile, and her infectious laughter became even louder. Intuitively, I knew she was scared, even though she put on a positive front.

Before she got sick with cancer, we had often been at odds with each other, because she found me too smart and difficult to control. In the United Kingdom our relationship became sweeter, and I felt she loved me more than she could express. She showed her love by showering me with gifts. I do not think she ever realized that spending time with her was the best gift she gave me.

The one thing that continued to cause friction between us was her relationship with my dad. As a sensitive thirteen-year-old, I felt torn between my parents and wished she would stop telling her family about his cruelty. When she started on one of her tirades, I would lock myself away in a room, which she took as a personal attack. She accused me of not loving her, because she thought I was siding with him. In truth, I felt so much pain about her illness and my dad's actions that I reacted by pulling away. I knew she was speaking her truth, but it was difficult for me to accept it. I did not understand her need to talk so she could heal. To this day, I harbor guilt that I was not as compassionate as I could have been. I was too young to understand what she was going through. In so many ways, I was a child.

Muhamed, the man I was to marry, did not see me as a child. He saw me as a possession he owned, a ripe, beautiful woman who was his to control. While I was in the United Kingdom, staying at my uncle's house, he constantly called from his apartment in New York City to check on what I was doing. Whenever he heard I was out with my male cousins, he accused me of immoral behavior and screamed at my sick mother. He acted crazy, and my mum had significant doubts about him. She felt something was off with him and knew our marriage would not work because of his intensely controlling nature.

Until then, she had ignored any red flags because he had showered my family and me with gold and jewelry. In the Gambia, displays of wealth are important and signify that a man can take good care of a wife. Now my mum saw his behavior as disrespectful to her and me. She was ready to cancel the marriage and arrange another match.

Let me be clear. My mum and dad did not believe there was any problem with forcing a young teen into marriage. They thought that it was the right thing to do and that they were fulfilling their responsibility as my parents. In my country, like in so many places in the world, arranged marriages are seen in a positive light, and you are considered an old maid if you are not married and have no children by the age of eighteen. My sisters were fourteen when they married, and three of the five of them are happy with their husbands. Nor did my parents have any issue with taking away my choice to find love. As Tina Turner sang, "What's love got to do, got to do with it? What's love but a secondhand emotion?"[3] Later in my life, I would fall intensely in love and would better understand those lyrics than I did then.

My family was complex and filled with contradictions. My parents and siblings loved me and were protective of me, but they saw no problem with either FGM or child marriages. It was part of our culture, and my father saw both practices as religious obligations. In my parents' eyes, I was the rebel.

While my intended husband was showing his true colors, my mum's health deteriorated. A few days before returning to the Gambia, we had a final visit with her doctor in London. She would not have let me accompany her if she had known what he would say. The doctor told her she was terminal, with only a few months left to live. She looked at me, and I pretended I had no idea what he was saying. When we left the hospital, she told me not to listen to doctors, since no one knows when another human will die. I told her I agreed with her, but deep down, I felt numb and empty inside. I saw her death coming.

We landed in the Gambia, and she quickly became sicker. After trying traditional herbal medicine, which caused bad side effects but no improvement, she returned to the United Kingdom to see if anything else could be done. This time, I stayed home. I believe when my mum left, she knew she would not be returning. I got to talk with her only on the phone, and not being by her side was excruciating. Fortunately, she was surrounded by family at the hospital, including two of my older sisters. Her last days were filled with love. But she herself was filled with anger and resentment toward my father and stepmother. She chose to die in a foreign country, away from him, because she did not want the people who had hurt her the most to see her die. She was a very proud woman.

My mum's biggest fear was not death but what would happen to her children when she died. Her particular concern was for me and how much trouble I would get into without her because I was strong-willed and curious. I also had a big heart, and she worried people would take advantage of my giving nature. She felt that my stepmother and my future husband would quash my spirit and that my dad would take away my independence, like he had taken away hers.

I was in school on the day my mum died, which was on October 20, 2004. My driver came to get me and said I needed to go home. My mother had bought a small car and had hired a driver to drive me to school daily because she felt education was important and wanted to remove any obstacles that might prevent me from attending. When I opened the car door and looked into the driver's eyes, I knew what had happened, but I refused to cry.

I walked into my home, went straight into the kitchen, picked up a knife, and started running after my stepmother. She was heavily pregnant, and I told her I wanted to kill her and her baby so she could experience my pain. People started screaming, and I was tackled and then locked in my room. Looking back at my actions, I realize that being raised in a home filled with violence, combined with my grief and the acute stress I endured from taking care of my mum, drove me to act in a way that was very unlike me. I am not violent, yet at that moment, all I felt was rage.

They sent my mum's body back to the Gambia for the funeral. It seemed like her entire family from Sierra Leone came for the burial, arriving a few days before her body did. Grieving, I walked into my mum's bedroom and saw her praying. I screamed. Then I found out this person was her eldest child, whom we had known nothing about. She was the spitting image of my mother. Imagine losing your mum and discovering you had a sister. It was just the first of the many shocks that awaited me in the upcoming months.

My dad was nowhere to be found. He was not there for my mum after he was told she was dying. Instead, he spent the entire month in Saudi Arabia to avoid being at her bedside and her funeral. His absence was extremely difficult for me and everyone who loved her. They saw it as him escaping his responsibilities and not wanting to face his guilt. They blamed my dad and stepmother for my mum's death. After she was buried, I did not want to stay in the house, eat the food they cooked, or communicate with anyone.

I hated life. My mum was right to be worried about me. After her death, I was lost. The friction in my family became unbearable. And I was so far behind in my studies, I did not get a good grade on an exam I needed to pass in order to move forward in school. My school had no compassion for a grieving teenager who had left the classroom to help her mother, and my family did not have the wealth and influence needed to change the school officials' minds. Thus, my opportunity for an education in the Gambia was over when I was fourteen, and my dad and sisters saw this as the right moment to send me to New York City to get married. Even though my mum had made it clear to my family that Muhamed was the wrong man for me, they did not listen.

Not wanting to deal with an outburst, my dad told me I was going on a short trip to New York City to help me escape my grief. No mention was made of marriage. I bought into his subterfuge because I was excited to get away to a place I had always dreamed about. That excitement immediately turned to fear and loathing when my intended husband met me at the airport in a fancy limousine, which he thought would impress me. He immediately started to grope and kiss me during the trip to my uncle's apartment in the Bronx, even though he saw nothing but disdain in my eyes and body language. Looking at him was so intimidating that I tried keeping my eyes down for most of the trip, barely getting a glimpse of the city I had heard so much about. I hoped that I would become invisible by avoiding his leering face and that he would leave me alone. He did not.

Now it is my wedding night, and I lie curled up tightly in his bed, having discovered that my genitals are mutilated beyond my comprehension and that the man I married cares absolutely nothing about me. Despite my physical pain, he stops pushing into me only when he hurts himself. I hide that my marriage is unconsummated from my family, hoping this will give me a way to end it.

They find out and decide to take me to a doctor in downtown Manhattan to be reopened so my husband can penetrate me. They realize I was infibulated, where the clitoris and labia are cut and the vagina is sealed, leaving only a tiny hole. When you are infibulated, you cannot have sex until you are cut back open.

My only thought is to escape. I run away but have nowhere to go. The streets of New York City are a terrifying place for a young teenage girl with no money and no experience surviving alone. Defeated, I return home that night. The next morning I am forced into a car and taken to the doctor, who cuts my vagina open during a painful operation. The doctor advises me to have sex immediately to keep the hole open. My husband shows only callousness. That very night, he takes me, and I experience the worst physical agony in my life. The women I know have never talked about the pain or revealed that sex is going to hurt forever. It is not a conversation we have. We have a culture of silence.

At fifteen, I am trapped with a man who sees me only as a beautiful young trophy who will satisfy him sexually and bear his children. No one in my family will protect me, because they see me as the troublemaker. All I can think about is returning home to Africa, despite knowing how difficult my life will be due to the disgrace I will bring my family. It does not matter. I yearn to become the Gambian girl of my childhood once again.

Chapter 2

The Gambian Girl

N O MATTER WHERE I LIVE or travel, the Gambia is home to me. Every time I step foot on the sandy soil of my country and breathe in the air, my heart grows bigger and beats faster. There is no place I love more. The Gambia is heaven here on earth, despite the poverty and the cruelty women and girls experience there.

The smallest country in mainland Africa, the Gambia measures less than thirty miles at its widest point and has a population of approximately 2.28 million people. It is named after the river Gambia, one of West Africa's major rivers. Stuck literally inside Senegal's "womb," the Gambia opens to the Atlantic Ocean, and this coastline has turned our little country into a strategic place for sea trade, transport, and exploitation. The Gambia is often confused with Zambia. That is probably why the article "the" came to rescue us: it was affixed to the country's name, distinguishing us from Zambia.

We are a bird-watcher's paradise, with close to six hundred species of birds and fifty miles of coastline. If you venture inland, you will see crocodiles and hippos residing in the river and monkeys chatting on hotel grounds. Beautiful beaches and wildlife are not our only claim to fame. The Gambia once stood at the center of the slave trade, as highlighted by Alex Haley in his bestselling book *Roots*, which ABC adapted as a television miniseries by the same name. Haley's great-great-grandfather is said to have been born in a village on the river Gambia, and Kunta Kinteh Island was once a major waypoint of the slave trade.

The Gambia is home to nine tribes. I am Serahule (also called

Soninke). The Serahule people are one of the oldest ethnic groups in Black Africa. We are known primarily as the founders and builders of the ancient Ghana Empire, which covered much of West Africa. The cultural identity of my tribe is very conservative, and it is viewed as a preserver of the norms and values that define the greater traditional ethos of our land. This conservatism is perhaps rooted in the leadership role my tribe once held in the region. This role became linked to a glorious past, and the collective memory of that past has bridged the old and modern worlds.

My people are segregated and classified by caste, wealth, and influence, with the Serahule usually marrying only people from their own tribe and caste. The caste you belong to represents how you are treated and looked at; that is no different from other caste systems you find worldwide. Among the Serahule, one caste is the peasant or slave class, known as the Kome. There is also the Hore caste, made up of those who are considered freeborn or nobles. I am part of the Hore caste, and I grew up in what is regarded as a noble family, one that "owned" people, who were considered our slaves.

My town of Gambissara, in the Upper River Region, is on the cusp of the Gambian countryside. Gambissara has about ten thousand people, mostly from my Serahule ethnic group. Many residents are farmers, who grow groundnuts, maize, and millet. These crops were introduced to fund colonialist enterprises, and this resulted in the groundnut becoming the main crop and depleting the soil of its minerals over the years.

Historically, our people have relied heavily on farming. Nowadays there are fewer farmers because of the poor soil quality, urbanization, and migration to the Gambia's urban centers and abroad. Over the years, the town's sons and daughters who traveled abroad have invested in Gambissara and modernized it to the extent that it now has fresh, modern buildings standing alongside a few grass huts. The ever-present friction between the traditional and the modern reflects itself in our architecture.

I was born on November 9, 1989, and spent my early years

in Gambissara with my aunts, uncles, and cousins in a big family compound. They lived in small concrete homes surrounding the big house, where my dad, his wives, and my multiple brothers and sisters lived. The mosque for the entire town was in the front part of our house. Like his father, my father was the Imam, the prayer leader, spiritual advisor, and expert on Islamic law for our community. Gambians are very religious, and our faith is mostly tied to the Islamic worldview, precepts, and beliefs.

Outside our house was a raised concrete platform, where everyone from the compound would sit and talk, especially when it was too hot to be inside. We cooked outside and had no indoor bathrooms, and sheep and goats roamed throughout the town. I remember a few dogs, although we did not own one. During a typical day, the kids ran around, sometimes with no clothes or shoes on, and we would play in the water while the women washed clothes. We attended religious school to learn about our faith and gathered together to share meals.

It was very dry where we lived, but out in the bush you would see many trees. The women were responsible for the peanut crops, while the men raised the millet and corn. Sometimes, I would go with my stepmother to our farm to climb trees and hunt birds. I loved hunting and grilling the birds, although I do not know why it was such a favorite pastime. I would also climb up the baobab trees, get the fruit, and use a stick to mix it with milk to make my Gambian version of ice cream.

Not from Gambissara, my grandfather had a huge cattle farm. I would travel there with my dad, drink fresh raw milk with dried millet, and eat mangos, oranges, and limes straight from the trees. These trips with my dad remain among my favorite childhood memories. Another favorite memory is going to the weekly market, to which traders came from other villages and towns, bringing things we did not usually have. I would get dressed up, and once at the market, I would gaze with excitement at all the colors, jewelry, and different foods on display.

While my childhood may have seemed good, there was a dark side, which I blocked out until recently because I could not handle talking or thinking about it. It is a trauma that continues to haunt me. Like every Gambian girl I have met—and there are thousands—I was constantly molested as a child. It seems to me everyone was molested by the men, who were often family members. They touched you at every opportunity and thought they could do whatever they wanted to the young girls. My mother and dad were frequently gone, and I was left at home with my half sister. One uncle would molest both of us when our parents were not around. Even though we were very young, we didn't believe we could say anything about it. We thought if we did, we would be punished severely. Adults afforded us no protection.

What happened back then is still happening today. Nobody talks about it. Many girls do not have a voice to say anything about molestation, FGM, or the reality of being a child bride. They are labeled rebellious and are beaten if they go against the cultural norms. Sometimes, they experience even worse. I vividly remember a young woman who was beaten to death by her family for becoming pregnant outside of marriage. Her father was my grandfather's brother and a Muslim extremist. There were no repercussions for committing this violent act, only silence.

When I was six, we left my birthplace to move to Serekunda, a city with one of the busiest highways and marketplaces in all of the Gambia. It was an exciting change for me because of the educational opportunities the move offered. My mum was adamant that her daughters attend school. One of my parents' fights was about educating her daughters, since education for girls was not part of my dad's tradition. I was the eighth of her nine children and the first to be enrolled in school, along with my sister. A very talkative child, I ensured everyone at school knew me from day one. I liked to answer all the questions, and people considered me bright. Maybe I was a bit of a teacher's pet, but being in the classroom was a joyous occasion.

Life in the city was good. In the evenings and on weekends, my sister Fatoumata and I would walk across town to the religious school, where we would see our friends and family. I would buy street food, a habit I love even today. For the first time, my family had a dog. He had been a pet of the previous tenants, who had rented the house from my dad. They took the dog with them, but he returned to our home, again and again. This dog was a mischief-maker who would follow my mum everywhere, including to the market. He would always take something from the stalls, like a stuffed animal. I did not know about pets, so I thought he was a bad dog for stealing.

We lived on one of the major highways where everything happened. I witnessed marches and demonstrations; if there was a coup d'état, it happened on that highway. When a coup d'état occurred in the Gambia in 1994, my dad, my grandmother, and I were in our city house, surrounded by the military. People could not leave their homes. My dad did not cook, so he fed me powdered milk. In fact, I loved this milk so much, I still drink the same brand today.

I would climb the wall around our house to see what was happening on the highway. I did not understand what was going on around me, since I was only five. As I got older, I sometimes would follow the marchers, out of curiosity. Not surprisingly, I always got in trouble with my parents when they found out about this. During one demonstration, students were shot in front of our house while trying to climb over our wall to escape. Even though I did not understand the politics, I firmly believed sending armed forces after kids just a few years older than me was wrong.

Although my family life and the outside world were intense, I adapted and flourished. I was engaged in my community and was always dancing and making friends. What was most exciting was developing my first close friendship. My friend's father was a prominent official, and she attended the most prestigious and expensive school in the Gambia. We were joined at the hip when we were not in the classroom. We learned how to cook and put on makeup, we read the novels teen girls loved, and we talked about boys.

I considered her my best childhood friend, and her betrayal of me later in my life with a man I loved deeply left me shattered in ways I could not imagine. I thought the bonds of friendship were sacred, and I could not believe women could be so vicious to other women, although I had witnessed it in my home, between my mum and my stepmother. I have always believed women have enough problems without turning on each other.

I was also highly aware of the disparity between my life and that of most people in my country. People would often come to our house and beg for food, even for the leftovers from our table. The most vulnerable were—and continue to be—girls and women. While I had the fortune of going to school and my family had drivers and maids, I saw girls being molested on the streets as they sold fruits or whatever they could to help support their families. Men pushed these girls up against walls, grabbed their breasts, slapped their ass, and groped them everywhere.

The irony is that Gambian girls' purity was—and still is— considered a necessary virtue. If they marry, girls need to be virgins. My father would boast that none of his daughters dishonored him by getting pregnant before marriage and that all were virgins. Rape is considered the girl's fault, and any chance of marriage and a family after that vanishes. And while the poor are the most vulnerable, young Gambian girls across all classes are constantly sexualized while having their sexual pleasure taken away. The ultimate example of this behavior is FGM.

I was only a week old when my parents arranged for me to get circumcised. In my family, when a girl was born, she was inevitably circumcised. My mum probably cried while I was being cut, but she thought she was doing what was right for me. My aunt and my sisters told me this was how we lived. There were no ifs, ands, or buts about it. I should never have been taught to accept those kinds of things.

The woman who cut me was my mother's friend. She thought it was the normal thing to do. I have since asked her why she did it. Her reason was that when I was born, they could tell from my eyes that I was strongheaded. They wanted to tame me and protect me from the promiscuity they forecast in my future.

Fundamentally, we live in world where all too often women are made to believe they must bow down to men. Men tell women they want their daughters cut, and it is done. Each year, millions of girls and women worldwide are at risk of undergoing FGM, a procedure carried out sometime between infancy and the age of fifteen. Though the practice varies from culture to culture, it carries serious psychological, socioeconomic, health, physical, emotional, and sexual consequences. There are three types of FGM. Type 1 involves the partial or total removal of the clitoris. Type 2 is the partial or complete removal of the clitoris and the labia (the inner and outer lips surrounding the vagina). Type 3 is the worst kind and is what was done to me—sewing the labia together to make the vaginal opening smaller.

While FGM is no longer legal in the Gambia, it is still practiced by some people. Most people who practice FGM see it as good and believe nobody has the right or the authority to tell them otherwise. They think that women who have gone through FGM are cleaner than those who have not. If you are a woman without FGM, you are not considered a woman. Many of my people believe FGM makes a woman whole. When a bride from another tribe or a country without FGM marries someone from a tribe that practices it, she is circumcised in order to become a real woman and to be accepted by her new family and community.

Some communities also view FGM as a religious practice, even though no religion condones violence against women and girls. The tribe I belong to practices it for religious reasons and does not have any ceremonies to accompany the cutting. Prayers are said in privacy by the mother and the woman who is doing the cutting. In contrast, the Mandinka tribe of West Africa considers the practice a rite of passage. Usually, the procedure is done on a group of girls, and the same knife is used on all of them. Most of the time, the blade is not even sterilized. After the cutting, the celebrations begin. Those who have gathered dance, cheer for the girls, and give them cash and gifts because they have "made it" to womanhood and are now considered clean and whole.

So many myths and misconceptions surround FGM. I encountered a young woman from my home village who genuinely believed a woman could not give birth unless she underwent FGM. Some think the clitoris can grow into a penis if left untouched. Others believe FGM helps curb a woman's desire for sex, making her more faithful to her partner. From their perspective, this practice is a way of ensuring a woman becomes a better spouse. It is astonishing how deeply ingrained these beliefs can be within specific communities. And while you and I may find these beliefs absurd, we must recognize that they form a significant part of these people's belief systems. Addressing these deeply rooted misconceptions and cultural beliefs is crucial in eradicating FGM. Sensitive and comprehensive education, awareness, and understanding are required to bring about positive change and to protect the rights and well-being of girls and women.

When I was about eight, one of my dad's wives had her first child, who was named Fatou after her maternal grandmother. A week after her delivery, an older woman came to our house. She was known as the circumcision lady because she had circumcised all the women in my family and was praised for her easy hand and skill. As the oldest wife, my mum was responsible for circumcision and other family rituals. When the old woman arrived, my mum directed her to my stepmother's room. I did not understand what was happening then, but I felt a heaviness and tension in the air. Though I was too young to understand, I remember how tiny and innocent my baby sister looked and how pretty she was. My mother brought a bowl of hot water and dry towels into the room and closed the door.

Curious, I pressed my ear to the door and could hear the old woman reciting from the Qur'an, the central religious text of Islam. Then there was a piercing scream from the baby. I heard the woman ask my mum to hold Fatou's legs open, and then she soothed my stepmother by telling her it was almost over. After ten minutes, the old woman finally left the room, but my sister continued screaming. My mum was told how to care for the wound.

The bleeding did not stop. My stepmother kept frantically asking my mum what to do. My mum relied on the expertise of the circumcision lady, who had told her that this was normal and that the bleeding would eventually stop. Hours passed, and my stepmother knew how weak her newborn had become. At last, she decided to rush her to the hospital. It was too late.

One of the worst things I have ever experienced was watching my innocent sister bleed to death. My family thought my sister died because it was God's will. It was as simple as that. They did not blame the practice of FGM. They used nice words to console my stepmother, but I cannot imagine the pain she felt over losing her first child. At the hospital, they asked her who had circumcised her daughter, but she refused to tell. Instead, she said my mum was responsible. As a result, my mum was reported to the police and called in for questioning, but FGM was not illegal in the Gambia at that time, so the police allowed her to go.

My mum was furious that my stepmother had thrown her under the bus, and they argued about who was responsible for the baby's death. I grew so tired of hearing their voices echoing throughout the compound day in and day out. Finally, I confronted them and told them they were both murderers and were equally responsible for my sister's death. My mum slapped me and accused me of being disrespectful.

This proud Gambian girl saw things differently than them. I still do. My mum thought me disrespectful, but I did not see it that way. While I believe everything happens by the will of God, certain things, like FGM, are not the will of God but of men. You would think my family would have realized this after what happened to Fatou. But a cultural norm is powerful and hard to break. Combating a religious belief is an even more challenging mountain to climb.

This is also true about child marriages. As a young woman growing up in the Gambia, I witnessed the devastating impact of child marriage in my country. And I lived through my two child marriages before I was eighteen—one forced on me and the other a choice, which I now see was not really a choice at all. I do know that child marriages are not only a violation of child protection and human rights, but they also negatively affect children's health and wellness and severely limit their opportunities in life.

As with FGM, many people believe child marriages are tied to being Muslim. That is a falsehood. According to many scholars, Islamic law fundamentally opposes child marriage, considering it marriage without consent.[4] Though no minimum age for marriage is stipulated in the Qur'an, having sound judgment and possessing maturity are clear preconditions to entering into a marital contract.

Poverty and a lack of education are fundamental reasons for child marriages. Families facing economic hardships may view marrying off their young daughters as a means of attaining financial security or settling debts. This perpetuates a cycle of poverty, as child brides are denied access to education and opportunities. When girls are educated, they gain the knowledge and confidence necessary to make informed decisions about their lives, including when and whom to marry. Girls who receive an education are less likely to marry before age eighteen.

Even though FGM and child marriages were outlawed in the Gambia in 2015 and 2016, respectively, they are still practiced. However, the numbers have gone dramatically down. In other parts of the world, children are not so fortunate, so the work of this Gambian woman continues in support of so many others who are fighting against these practices.

This work has been particularly challenging for me as a Muslim woman. Both my parents were deeply spiritual and ensured that I received a solid Islamic education. Religion has always been integral to my life, deeply interwoven with my family and upbringing. Growing up in a household headed by an Imam and in a home housing a mosque allowed me to engage easily in daily prayers. During my early years, I prayed without fully comprehending the deeper meaning behind the rituals.

Today my spirituality ebbs and flows. There are times when I feel an intense connection with the higher power, and there are moments when I question everything, which leads me to a temporary disconnect from religious practices. Ramadan always rejuvenated my spiritual side. I found joy in joining my father, my brothers, and the rest of my family in prayer during the holy month. The community aspect of worship held greater significance for me than individual acts of prayer. Being surrounded by family, neighbors, and fellow believers made the experience more meaningful and fulfilling.

As a young girl, I was not required to attend the mosque daily like the boys. My father, though religious, was not demanding when it came to our religious practices. While some households may have had stricter expectations, ours had a more relaxed approach to religious adherence. This upbringing allowed me to explore and develop my relationship with spirituality at my own pace. As I grew older, I started to distinguish between religion and spirituality. For me, spirituality represents a belief in a higher power and a sense of being loved and guided by something divine. However, I wonder if religious rituals are the exclusive gateway to experiencing this spiritual connection.

Religion and spirituality became intertwined in my activism against such harmful practices as FGM and child marriage. Working with religious leaders opened my eyes to the complexities of tackling these issues while also respecting cultural and religious sensitivities. My spiritual journey allowed me to question and critically examine specific aspects of religious texts and teachings, especially regarding FGM. I have tried to dispel misconceptions and emphasize that FGM is more cultural than religious. My work in this area has challenged people's perceptions and earned me respect and recognition from some scholars and religious leaders, and fury and condemnation from others.

Child marriage, however, presents a more formidable challenge, as it is deeply ingrained in various cultures worldwide. I have trod carefully while advocating against this practice, acknowledging its historical roots while striving to create awareness and change.

In pursuing gender equality, I firmly believe that understanding the role of religion and faith is crucial. Religion profoundly impacts our identities and influences societal norms and practices. By appealing to the humanity of religious leaders, I hope to pave the way for a more compassionate and equitable world. My journey with religion and spirituality has been dynamic and enlightening. It has allowed me to embrace faith, question religious teachings, and work toward a more just and inclusive society. While spirituality remains a constant in my life, my perspective on religion continues to evolve as I learn more and grow in my understanding of faith and its role in shaping our lives.

My mum always said that she knew when she looked into my eyes when I was an infant that I would be a different kind of Gambian girl. She was right. That observation became a reality when I came to America. But, unfortunately, she was no longer there to protect me.

Chapter 3

Coming to America

EXCITEMENT BUBBLED INSIDE ME as I boarded the plane to New York City. The prospect of stepping onto a land I had heard about only in stories and seen only on the big screen filled me with an indescribable thrill. America was a place of dreams and opportunities, and I was ready to experience it. The flight was long, and my heart raced with anticipation. I could not wait to see the city that never slept, the towering skyscrapers, and the bustling streets portrayed in countless films. My mind was a canvas painted with vivid images of a world beyond my own, a world I was about to become a part of.

After the plane's wheels touched the ground in New York on Christmas Day, something shifted inside me, and my initial excitement wavered. I never anticipated my husband-to-be, a man who was at least twenty years older than me and whom I barely knew, would pick me up at the airport. I quickly realized that this short trip my father had arranged to help me heal from my mum's death was all about solidifying my marriage to Muhamed. I was expected to greet him with a warm hug, chat during the car ride, and smile on cue. Yet all I felt was discomfort, a lingering unease. I was disgusted when he tried to kiss me and then criticized my family for my reaction. All he wanted to do was touch me, and I kept hitting him to get him to stop.

But Muhamed was only part of my disillusionment. As we drove straight to my aunt and uncle's home in the Bronx, I realized the images of the city I carried in my imagination were far from the reality. The streets were not paved with gold; I encountered a dirty urban landscape. The American dream I had envisioned seemed distant as the snow-covered roads we traveled quickly turned into messy slush. New York City's melting snow created a muddy river flowing across the pavements, and navigating through it was daunting. The freezing temperatures only added to my discomfort, and I could not help but compare the New York winter to the Gambia's pleasant climate.

I was also taken aback by the stark contrast between my life in the Gambia and the living conditions in the cramped, tiny apartment my aunt and uncle called home. My family in the Gambia was not accustomed to extreme poverty, but my family in America resided in public housing, where rats and roaches seemed to have taken over. The reality of this environment made me long for the comfort and familiarity of my homeland.

When we arrived at the apartment, people were busy talking and cooking. At one point during the evening, Muhamed came over to me with a number of his friends, who gushed over his "new, young, beautiful wife." I tried fending off his groping hands and his kisses throughout the evening, and my family thought I behaved badly. They were not at all disgusted by his behavior and were surprised by mine. Fortunately, they decided to put the wedding off so I could adjust to my new circumstances.

I was sent to Atlanta to live with one of my sisters and her husband. I fell in love with the city, which was much cleaner and warmer than New York. School had not yet resumed, so I wandered around and enjoyed a new part of America, which came closer to what I had dreamt about. To pass the time, I also joined an online chat group, where I met a Gambian boy named Jamil, who lived in New Jersey. We developed an instant rapport and soon began talking every day. Despite the distance, we started "dating," much to my family's disapproval. They would not give me a cell phone, so Jamil and I generally communicated online. Of course, they had no problem forcing me to talk to Muhamed, who constantly called me.

I finally enrolled in the eleventh grade and was eager to start a new chapter in my life. However, it did not go as smoothly as I had hoped. My heavy accent made me stand out in the classroom, and I was often asked to repeat myself. I persevered, made supportive friends, and threw myself into my coursework. I was determined to excel. Then Muhamed came to visit me, and once again, I was subjected to his physical advances. Despite my progress in school and the happiness I had found in Atlanta, my family decided it was time for the marriage ceremony. When I told the school guidance counselor from my previous school in New York City what was going to be done to me, she did not believe me.

I was forcibly returned to New York. On the night of my wedding, my family prepared me for the ceremony. I cried so much and pleaded with my dad. I begged. It made no difference. An older woman who was like a sex adviser came to tell me what to do—which position to assume to make it more comfortable and which products to use to lessen the pain. She bathed me and smoothed scented lotion all over my body. Then they dressed me in white lingerie and waist beads.

I was locked inside a room to prevent my escape until I was handed over to my husband. I was forced to kneel before him. Then everyone left so Muhamed could consummate the marriage. Before he could touch me, I rushed into the bathroom and locked the door behind me. I slept in the bathtub that night, but I could not elude him forever. Two weeks later he violated me on our "marriage" bed. I cried the whole time, particularly for my mum, because I felt she would have saved me if she had been there.

During those dark days, my only lifeline was Haddy, my childhood friend from the Gambia, Later, when a documentary about my life was produced, she said, "After Jaha got married, we would call each other all the time. While she was there, it was constant crying. She was fifteen, and she was expected to be a wife. The guy would threaten her with violence. It was just awful for her."

One day I called my old school guidance counselor again. This time, she believed me when I told her what was happening to me, and she put me in touch with Equality Now, an organization whose mission is to protect and promote the rights of women and girls. Someone at Equality Now coached me on what to do. That evening I told Muhamed that if he laid a hand on me again, I would call the police. Furious, he beat me and took away my phone, thinking my resistance would break in a few days. But I refused to back down. I still do not know where I got the strength to stand up to him.

My husband sent me back to my uncle's house, hoping my family would pressure me to change my attitude. Finally free from the confines of Muhamed's apartment, I contacted Equality Now again and asked for more help. Meanwhile, my family was furious with me and even allowed my husband to come to the house and do whatever he wanted to me. After all, I was now a married woman.

Unable to handle my family's fury and my husband's behavior any longer, I headed to Equality Now's offices in Manhattan. There I was introduced to Taina Bien-Aimé, a founding board member of the organization and later its executive director, who in 2014 became the executive director of the Coalition Against Trafficking in Women. Despite what my family said, Taina showed me that what was happening to me was not normal or okay. We developed a strong relationship, and she became my guardian angel. I do not doubt she is the reason I am alive today.

In the documentary recounting my fight to have FGM abolished, Taina shared her perspective on this time in my life: "I kept telling her if you can escape, there is a police station down your block, or come to the office or my home. It was an emotional tug-of-war she was going through. 'How can I extricate myself from this violence without totally divorcing my family or without turning my back on everything I know?'"

Taina connected me with Sanctuary for Families, an organization dedicated to aiding victims of domestic violence and their children. She and the people at Sanctuary quickly became my found family and got to work to help me. First, they assisted me with adjusting my immigration status so I could legally stay in the United States. They also gave me clothes, as I had left Muhamed's house with nothing.

As Taina and Sanctuary worked to help me, Muhamed told my family he wanted to take my sister and me on a trip to New Jersey. Scared to say no and hoping to see Jamil, who had been a source of comfort and support for me, I agreed to go. Once we arrived at our destination, I convinced my sister to let me go see a "friend from school," leading her to believe it was a girl. I snuck off to meet with Jamil instead, and on that occasion, I also met his parents, who had only compassion for a frightened fifteen-year-old girl. Jamil and his family were immensely supportive and never judged me. As it turned out, Jamil played a significant role in my life during this crucial period. In many ways, he was the catalyst for my pursuit of an education. His dedication to learning inspired and motivated me.

When I returned from meeting Jamil, my husband took me to see his family, who tried to convince me to return to my marriage. I pretended to acquiesce, fearing what they might do if I refused. But once back in New York, I made it clear that I would not return to Muhamed. He and my family became furious, but I stood my ground, insisting I wanted to attend school instead. They scoffed at the idea, but I would not be deterred. I was determined to escape and leave him permanently, and I had decided the only way to do it was by finishing my education.

Less than a year after my marriage began, I was divorced. I was able to convince my family that because Muhamed had suffered an accident before our marriage that left him with a head injury and a broken back, under Islamic law, I could leave the marriage. I was not obligated to stay married to him because of his disabilities.

After my marriage ended, my life continued to be hellish. It seemed like everyone looked at me like I had disgraced my family. The exception was my uncle, who had also been there for my mother when she moved from Sierra Leone to the Gambia. My mother had reciprocated by supporting my uncle when he immigrated to America. While my uncle tried to do his best at this time, our culture was such that he had little power to support me, other than giving me a place to stay and encouraging me.

Because this time in my life was so painful, all my thoughts turned to getting an education. As the school term rapidly approached, I could not contain my eagerness to return to school in the Bronx. I knew education was vital for my future, and I was determined to enroll in a good school. So I embarked on a mission to visit every school in the area to secure my enrollment. However, my hopes were dampened when I was repeatedly told the same disappointing news: I needed a legal guardian to be able to enroll. It felt like an insurmountable barrier, as I had no one to fulfill that role.

One day, when I reached the last school on my list, I felt disheartened and emotionally drained. When the school's administration echoed the exact same requirement for attendance, I could no longer hold back my emotions. Tears streamed down my cheeks as I poured out my story to the school's staff, explaining my situation and my challenges. I left the school feeling defeated. To my astonishment, I received an unexpected call from the school the next day. The principal had heard my story and had made an exception, allowing me to enroll. It was a moment of overwhelming joy and relief. With a heart full of gratitude, I headed to Taina and Sanctuary, where they graciously provided me with enough resources to purchase the school supplies I needed.

My dream of returning to school had not been shattered. Free of my husband, and with the support of a newfound family, I was on my way. But it would not be easy. I had no money and little family support. And as a new immigrant, I faced many challenges other people did not experience.

Chapter 4

The Immigrant Girl

ONE OF THE THINGS I LOVE MOST about America is chocolate. When I first came here, I drank Nesquik chocolate milk daily. I also loved chocolate chip cookies and pizza. I was never able to eat fast food, because it made me nauseous, but chocolate milk, candy, cookies, and pizza were always things I loved. Candy was not easily accessible in the Gambia.

I had very little money, but I enjoyed buying clothes, going to the movies, and getting my hair styled. I would save every dollar and then would spend ten dollars to get my hair blown out by a Dominican hairstylist in the Bronx. It made me feel pretty. Often I would hang out when the streets in my neighborhood came alive with children playing at open hydrants. These experiences were different from what I had known back in the Gambia.

While I lived with my aunt and uncle in New York City, I did not wear traditional African clothing. My attire during those years resembled that of typical American teenagers: jeans and casual tops. This often placed me in the crosshairs of judgment by my community, which expected me to adhere to traditional African norms. Despite the criticism, I never acquiesced to their expectations. Between school and work, my schedule left little time for the mosque or other community activities. This furthered my isolation, making me feel like an outcast. I was straddling two worlds and belonged to neither.

I had studied English in the Gambia but was not fluent when I arrived in the United States. My accent was pronounced, and my fellow classmates would make fun of my pronunciation. When I answered questions, sometimes the whole class would laugh. I always felt different at school, but fortunately, I made a few friends, such as the Jamaican boy I went to prom with. I was also a member of the track-and-field team.

Having come to the United States on a visitor visa, I became one of the countless faces of undocumented immigrants. It was not a label I wore with pride. Although my uncle and aunt gave me a place to sleep, I received no financial support from my family after I left my husband. At fifteen, I had to rely on odd jobs to keep afloat. I found myself hanging clothes at a shop in Manhattan, serving at a Jewish event site in Brooklyn, and cleaning toilets and offices. The jobs were not glamorous but were a means to an end. I worked hard.

Many jobs paid me in cash, and often employers did not even bother to find out my real name. They did not care. You just gave them whatever name you dreamt up, and they would hire you. They paid no heed to my age and my immigration status. Instead, they saw an opportunity to exploit cheap labor without providing any benefits, such as health care. It did not matter. I had a job. I went to work for whoever would hire me.

Being an illegal immigrant is scary, and exploitation is rampant. In 2005 the social climate did not seem as bad as it is today. President George W. Bush called for a more compassionate immigration system and recognized that the American economy could thrive by valuing immigrants. He saw immigrants as ambitious and hard-working people pursuing the American dream. That is certainly who I was, but it still did not stop the feeling of being powerless, less than, and fearful.

Fortunately, I had people in my corner. Taina and Sanctuary for Families helped me seek asylum, because I feared if I returned to the Gambia, I would be forced into marriage again. After my asylum was approved, I applied for a green card and citizenship in 2015. I felt genuinely American when I received my citizenship. It was interesting because at that time, I was wearing traditional clothing and covering my head due to my work in the Atlanta community. I looked more African while feeling more American. Now I hold dual citizenship in the United States and the Gambia.

Sometimes, we fail to understand what people go through as immigrants and what they need to survive whatever hardships they have fled. My story is not different from the stories we hear from people trying to seek refuge in this country, better their lives, and live the American dream we hear about so often. They do not realize what it takes to live that dream or the scars one accumulates trying to get there.

I think immigration is even more challenging for women. The Gambian men I knew who had immigrated to America had some freedom to seek job opportunities, while women were expected to stay home and care for their children. Many did not speak English. Even today I see the challenges many immigrant women face, how they end up living in poverty and relying on social services. I am concerned about immigrants settling in impoverished, violent communities and the effects this has on their children. However, I also understand that they live in such communities due to financial constraints.

Most immigrants believe life will be better in America. That is why they come here. But the reality is often different. Out of shame, some do not return home when their expectations do not match their experiences. They keep trying to succeed but often find it challenging to make progress. There is a perception that life will be much better in a different country. But the reality for many immigrants is that life is not necessarily better. They do not make it big, build a house, and send money back to their family.

I am fortunate. I am the fulfillment of that American dream in every aspect—from where I come from to where I am today and the kind of work I do. I believe anyone can come to this country and become whatever it is they want. My education is from America. The people I met here believed in me when my family did not.

American doctors took care of me when I struggled because of the trauma I had experienced. Part of me will always see America as home. All of me will always be filled with gratitude.

Yet I also feel sorrow that I needed to leave my birthplace, as did all my siblings who emigrated. The Gambia and other African nations need to keep their people there. One reason I am involved in development issues, such as transportation, job creation, and technology, is to show people in Africa that you can stay home and make it. You do not have to travel across the sea to live that dream. Africa has so much potential, but many people view it as a place where you cannot make it, and the poverty levels are so extreme. They see people like me who were fortunate to go to the United States and build better lives. They do not believe us when we say Africans can make it in Africa.

I believe strongly that African governments need to use their power to provide opportunities so that people do not leave the continent. I believe we have a moral responsibility to transform Africa into something much better than the one we inherited. Then people will not need to leave their families and go to other countries in order to survive and thrive. I will discuss some ideas about how to change this mindset later in the book.

My experiences as an immigrant molded me into the person I am today. My immigrant status made me feel hope and fear at the same time. It made me go after opportunities and overcome challenges. The complexity of living in two cultures—Gambian and American—was often confusing and caused conflict inside me and with my family. Reflecting back, I realized that enduring FGM, being a child bride, and immigrating to America shaped me as a survivor.

My parents were perhaps the force that had the most profound effect on me—both the good and the bad. I suspect many of you have experienced that in your own lives. What further complicated my relationship with them was the culture of my country and the politics, religion, and polygamy that structured everyday life and the roles individuals had to play.

I have learned we sometimes forget our parents are human beings, trying their best to live within the constraints of their world and personal histories. As I grew and then became a mum myself, I saw my parents in a new light, a more compassionate light. This made me determined to help create a world where parents treat their daughters with respect and honor. A world where sexual abuse, rape, genital mutilation, and forced marriages are no longer tolerated. A world where girls can dream big and become anything they want. A world where women have the education and financial stability that allows them and their families to thrive. Understanding my own parents has deepened my understanding of my own humanity.

Chapter 5

My Mum, My Dad

I HAVE SHARED MY MOTHER'S FIGHT with breast cancer and her tumultuous relationship with my dad. But she was so much more than that. Physically, she was beautiful, tall, and powerfully built, with one of those faces you never forget. Her dark skin and moon-bright teeth reflected the beauty of African women. She could have been a model. Beyond her arresting features and stature, she was a strong fighter who set the tone in her dealings with others. She created her path, a legacy I embrace. And what a personality she had. You could hear her laughter from miles away; when she was happy, she would sing and dance. While her physical beauty was rare, she was even more beautiful on the inside. She was a woman with empathy and the desire to help others. I inherited her compassion, strength, and maybe some of her cooking skills. Everyone around me says I act just like her. Quite simply, my mum had swag.

Originally from Sierra Leone, she grew up as an only child, and her mother died very young. She never discussed her upbringing, but I suspect things were tough for her when she was a child and a young woman. She probably never imagined she would end up in a rural village in the most distant part of the Gambia. Her reason for this was love. It is not lost on me that my parents did not allow me to marry for love, yet it was the driving force behind their union. My dad married my mother despite strong objections from his family. He remained very much in love with her even after a second wife joined our household.

My dad's family disliked my mum from the start and made her

life hell during the first decade of their marriage. They had already chosen a wife for him, but he decided to marry my mum, anyway. When the family elders heard they had married, they beat him for going against their wishes. My family members have told me that my parents fought hard for their love and remained in Sierra Leone for several years after they got married so they did not have to experience the animosity of my dad's family. They moved back to the Gambia only after my grandfather's health began to fail.

My mother's role as the first wife included caring for my paternal grandfather, even though he and my grandmother would not even talk to her. Over the years, their dislike turned to respect. By the time my grandfather died in 1989, the year I was born, he and my mum had become best friends because of the kindness and generosity she displayed as his primary caregiver. My grandfather always reminded my dad that a woman was not what she showed you but what went on in her heart, and my mum had the best of hearts.

After my family returned to the Gambia, my dad's uncle gave him one of his daughters to take as a second wife. This match was forced on him, and he and his new wife never connected. It was common knowledge that my dad loved my mum more than his wife. When you went to our home, the second wife and her kids were invisible in our family. That remains true to this day. To this day, my father is not close to these children, nor do they have the kind of strong relationship my mum's children have with him. This makes me feel very sad.

Regardless, my mum struggled with the idea of a second wife; she was a jealous woman who had never agreed with polygamy. You just had to look at her and you knew she did not feel happy about sharing her husband. As a child, I hated that my dad had other wives and other kids, because I felt like they took time away from me and my mum.

My dad went to Sierra Leone with his new bride to escape my mum's jealousy, leaving her behind with four little kids. Although she did not speak of it, this was one of the most challenging times in her life, because she was abandoned in a community where she did not know the language and where everyone looked at her suspiciously, and because her in-laws actively disliked her. The only thing my mum had going for her was her cooking and her generosity of spirit. A remarkable cook, she loved to give people food. And she was still deeply in love with my father. When my dad and his second wife returned to the Gambia, we made the move from our village to Serekunda. This made my mum happy because she had grown up in a city in Sierra Leone, and she viewed cities as places filled with opportunities, both financial and educational.

My mum was an excellent businesswoman, and she only partially relied on her husband financially. Back in the village, people remember her selling fish and palm oil in the market while holding me in her arms. In the city, she became more creative and innovative in her business ventures. She ended up with a good livelihood making and selling clothes to African diaspora communities in the United States and Europe.

Because I had a much lighter complexion, many could not fathom how I, that baby in her arms, was her child. My own skin tone never attracted any negative attention, but my mother was harassed because of the stark contrast in our skin tones. People sometimes suspected she had kidnapped me. She ended up cutting my hair so I would look more like her. As I grew up, my lighter skin tone generally conferred privileges upon me in Africa, including preferential treatment in various competitions and leadership roles in school. This is because lighter skin was often equated with beauty.

My dad took a third wife a few years after we moved to the city. She was the same age as my mum's third child, which made it even harder for my mum to accept. I have no idea why he wanted a third wife, except that having someone much younger than him was probably exciting. Unfortunately, this new addition reshaped my family in negative ways. I believe that my stepmother came with a competitive attitude toward my mum and lacked basic human respect, probably because she was so young. My new stepmother made it her job to get on my mum's nerves all the time. Consequently, the atmosphere in our house went from being peaceful to volatile, as fights and arguments erupted every day.

Around this time I began to notice my dad's abusive nature. My mum and my stepmother would fight, and my dad would side with his young wife. I was only eight at the time, but I clearly remember the change in my parents' relationship. This change ushered in the end of what I perceived to be a fairy-tale romance. By the time I was old enough to understand what was happening, *love* was not the word I would use to describe my parents' relationship. *Hatred*, *betrayal*, and *violence* were better descriptors. I wish I had been one of my parents' first children, so I could have witnessed more of the love and happiness between my parents.

One consequence of my mum's frustration with her life and with my father was she could be furious and violent. I spent much of my time trying to make her happy by buying her little gifts and doing errands for her. Most people around us thought I was her favorite, because she did not scold or hit me. In truth, it was because I had mastered the skills of avoiding confrontation and knowing what to say to get people to calm down and change their mind. When I was a child, my siblings sometimes disliked me for always knowing how to talk to my mum and dad when I needed something. For instance, my dad kept a tight hold on his purse, and often I was the only one who could get money from him. All my siblings, half-siblings, and their mothers would send me to him when they needed something.

My relationship with my father created a peculiar dynamic in that I could insult my stepmother whenever she disrespected my mum, knowing my dad would not lay a hand on me. Whenever my dad gave her money for household expenses and she sent me to do the shopping, I would conveniently "forget" to give her back the change. It was my silent rebellion, a way to reclaim some power when I felt powerless. My dad would dismiss her complaints about me, excusing my actions as those of a misunderstood child. This brought happiness to my mum's eyes, and in those rare moments, she would sing and dance around the house. Our shared joy infuriated my stepmother, who seemed to resent any happiness my mum and I found together.

I was mischievous in many ways. I caused trouble at home because I knew my dad would not punish me. Some people claimed I was not as well disciplined as my other siblings, because my parents allowed me to say and do whatever I pleased. My mum, however, allowed this only when I was on her side, while my dad saw me as an innocent child who could do no wrong.

I was constantly caught in the middle between my parents. When my stepmother married my dad, he basically "gave" me to her, telling her that I had the "cleanest heart in the house" and that she should keep me close. This designation as "good" created a great sense of responsibility and burden in me from an early age. I felt like I could not be angry or hold malice. And it remains that way to this day. I cannot fail. I cannot cry. I will always find a solution. I am the peacemaker and the sensible one, no matter what is going on. But I am human and not this constantly strong woman others want to believe in.

My father "giving me" to my stepmother deeply angered my mother. Yet despite her resentment of the new situation, she was intent on fulfilling one of her main goals: making sure her children became educated. Education was important to her because she came from a highly educated family. She enrolled my sister and me in school, but my dad would not pay for our studies, because he did not support the idea of his children getting a Western education. Not giving up, my mum used the money she earned on our schooling and was so proud when we went off that first day. She took pictures to send to her other children and her friends. My mum continued to support our education through her various side hustles, ensuring we lived a comfortable life and had everything we needed. When I finished grade school and entered middle school, she went a step further and enrolled me in one of the best private schools in the country.

My mum always knew I needed an educational foundation to achieve my destiny. Still, she could not envision that I would go far and make an impact, because I was a woman. Despite her strength and skills, it was beyond her comprehension that a woman could achieve what I have. So, she was torn between encouraging me and squashing my dreams. That is where our relationship became complex. While my mum loved me deeply, I felt that part of her hated me. I do not know if it was because she felt trapped in her own life. Because I was only fourteen when she died, neither of us had the opportunity to understand each other fully. Yet I am completely convinced she wanted her children to have opportunities and not end up living the life she had.

As the years went by before I moved to America, the tensions between my stepmother and my mum escalated, and their arguments became more frequent. It was a challenging environment to grow up in, and I often sought refuge outside our tumultuous home. Instead of enduring the constant bickering, I sought solace in school and various after-school programs. I became a regular participant in study groups and extracurricular activities, spending most of my free time away from home. During this time, I joined an organization called Lend a Hand Society, which was within walking distance of my school. There I met Haddy, who became my best friend, as well as others who helped shape my worldview at a young age. Lend A Hand gave us skills we are using to this day, such as organizing, public speaking, and fundraising skills. By participating in radio, television, and talent shows at Lend a Hand, I developed confidence in public speaking.

Despite our difficulties, my mum found me amusing, even though she rarely expressed it. She would boast about me to her friends wherever she went. My siblings sometimes teased her, claiming she was scared of me, because she never wanted me to be mad at her. I do not know if this is true, because my mum has remained a mystery to me. I recently had a conversation with a close friend of my mum's that gave me some revelations.

Isatou, as she was called by locals, met my mother when she was a Peace Corps volunteer in my village before I was born. The Peace Corps is a US organization whose mission is to promote world peace and friendship by sending trained volunteers to countries that need development assistance. The volunteers live and work side by side with community members on locally prioritized projects, building relationships and exchanging cultural capital and knowledge.

Isatou painted a vivid picture of my mum, describing their instant connection and how my mum embraced her like a lifelong friend. She knew all about me, and my mum had even shared with her pictures of my first day of school, including one with my mum in the frame. She said my mum was a Renaissance woman ahead of her time and believed in equal opportunities for her children, both boys and girls. She wanted us to be educated and to experience the world. Isatou and I discussed sensitive topics, such as female genital mutilation and child marriage. She revealed that my mum had felt powerless in those situations but had never wanted either of those for her children. She also told me my mother would be very proud of my work.

As I reflect back, I realize my parents did not know what to do with me. My mum thought I was too wild and feared what I would do or say next. She was worried I would never fit into this world. While she was very strict, she was more lenient with me than with my siblings. She laughed when I came home one day and told her, "I would never marry a guy with another wife. I would never let my husband hit me." My statements were disrespectful, given her situation, but she allowed me to have that view. Perhaps it was because she saw a light in me and believed I was the child who would rescue her. I am sure if she had lived, it would be beyond her wildest dreams that I am a political leader and a global women's rights activist.

Back then, my parents gave me mixed messages about what it meant to be a woman. My mother was a strong and independent woman with excellent skills as a businesswoman. Yet she was deeply concerned about my independent nature. My father is now one of my biggest cheerleaders, but he wanted me to be nothing more than a good daughter, a wife, and a mother. I remember him sitting outside our home and being serenaded by a praise singer about his ancestors' greatness. At the same time, I stood fanning him, as if he were a king.

My father has said that his strong bond with me is due to the fact that I have the purest heart among all his children. He and my family were certain that my unwavering support of them would not change, because of my pure heart. Again, this belief shaped me from a very early age. I was nicknamed "Super Basa" even before I had learned to walk, when I was two and half years old. (Basa, also called Bazeen, is a material used to make tie-dyed cloth, which is known for never losing its color or fading.) By the time I was walking, I knew how to have full conversations with people and loved to sing my nickname.

I have also heard rumors that my father's financial success came with my birth and that I was his lucky talisman. In fact, out of his thirty-three children, I proudly held the title of his favorite, a fact he once shared with anyone who would listen. Whatever the case, we have always been very close. Looking back, I remember nothing wrong between us, except when it came to how he treated my mum. He would always spend time with me and shield me from anyone who tried to scold me. Despite the complexities and challenges of my childhood, my relationship with my dad remains strong. And our bond grows stronger with each passing day.

I make no excuses for how badly my father hurt my mum. Yes, he was a product of his culture and acted within the boundaries of his rights as a man as he understood them. However, his behavior toward my mum was inexcusable. It had a negative effect on me and my siblings. After my mum's death, my father took on the role of both father and mother to her children. I particularly felt this attention and love.

As he has grown older, he has talked about his relationship with my mum and has deep regrets. He speaks very fondly of her, but when I and my siblings were younger, we never heard that. Sometimes, he stares at my sister, who looks just like my mum. Now we understand the love story they had, but it makes me very sad that things went so badly between them. I wish I had not seen the hate. A part of me really wishes my mum was still here, so she could understand how much he regrets his behavior and that he did love her. As for me, his revelations have brought me some comfort, but mainly confusion. Nothing is clear.

While my personality resembles my mum's, my looks do not. I look like my dad, with a similar height, skin tone, and features. No one would ever mistake him for anyone other than my father. He believes I am just like him. To some extent, that is true. My diplomatic skills come from him. He is a prominent Imam, a leader in the Soninke tribe, and a powerful man in the diamond-trading industry. He knows how to listen and speaks in a quiet but convincing manner. People trust and admire him for his knowledge, wisdom, and conduct. I have tried to emulate his style in my work as an activist, and I believe this is a primary reason why I have been effective. Recently, I also learned my father financially supports thousands of people in the Gambia. While they were growing up, none of his children knew that about him. I like to think my own generosity comes from him.

As an adult, I knew I had to address my parents' volatile relationship, along with my mutilation, my child marriages, the abuse I suffered, and the threats I received, which became a constant part of my life after I became a public figure. I went into therapy, which is uncommon among people from the Gambia. Therapy is neither culturally nor financially an option for most people in Africa, even though depression is recognized as a silent epidemic there, especially for women. What a contrast to the United States, where almost a quarter of the population is in therapy. Since I live in both worlds, I finally took the step to improve my mental well-being, a topic I will explore later.

My therapist concluded that what I had undergone in my life had resulted in post-traumatic stress disorder (PTSD) and treated me accordingly. I discovered that my attempt to distance myself from my memories and act like I had not been there did not mean I had not experienced and witnessed horrendous things that had consequences for my psyche. One of my most profound realizations was that my mum was my first bully. The loss of her when I was a young teenager had made me remember only the good things about her. She became the heroine in a tragedy, and my father, the villain. But in truth, it was my mum whose anger took the form of violence. My father never hit me and rarely spanked his other children. My mother, on the other hand, took out her frustrations on her children.

I had not realized before therapy that my mum's actions intensely affected how I saw myself. In therapy, I had flashbacks of my mum beating my older sister and even putting hot pepper in her vagina as a punishment. As a young girl, I witnessed my mum's behavior, which made me afraid. I did everything to avoid my mum, including staying away from my house as much as possible.

After my first therapy session, I called two of my older sisters to ask them if what I had recollected in therapy accurately reflected who my mum was. One sister started crying as soon as I started speaking. For the first time in our lives, we had an honest conversation about our mum. We had never had such a talk before because we came from a society where parents were always right. It did not matter what they did or said; our parents could do no wrong.

This sister hated me for most of my life because she thought I was the reason she never had our parents' love. I was the "perfect" child and did everything the way my parents wanted. I never received the beatings she received from my mum. But I did not escape without wounds. Even though I do not remember getting beaten by my mum, she did make fun of me, commenting, for instance, about how big my eyes were and how I looked like a frog. She praised me only when I did something nice for her, and she continuously compared me to my siblings if she was happy with me. This created a great deal of sibling rivalry. I do not think my mum knew how much her actions hurt us, and I am certain they made us who we are today.

My sister became the perfect wife as an adult, doing everything she could to keep her husband always happy and never going against his wishes. I became global Jaha, wanting to change the world no matter what the consequences were for me. Instead of taking my mother's anger and channeling it into violence, even as a child, I was the protector. I fought for my mum when I was old enough to understand the injustice she was enduring at home at the hands of my dad and his wife. If I was home and saw something, I would get involved. On days my mum was happy, I was always the child who joined her dancing.

Listening to Isatou's stories and going through therapy made me wish my mum was still alive so I could get to know her on a deeper level as a woman. Every day, I long for her support and her presence in my life. Those of us who lost our mothers before we became adults never get to experience how this relationship grows from the respect that comes with our maturity. Oftentimes, our mothers are not there when we need them the most. Hearing my mother's voice during my difficult marriages and my emergence as a public figure and activist would have eased much of the pain I went through. I so wish she could meet her grandchildren. Most importantly, I have never gotten answers to essential questions, particularly about why she vented so much of her anger and frustration on her children.

My relationships with my mum and dad are complicated, and my connections with my siblings are equally confusing. Over the years, they went from not understanding why I was different to gradually accepting me. My eight siblings, that is, the ones with whom I share the same mother, eventually came around and embraced me, but it took time. I always felt like my parents had given birth to perfect children who adhered to all the traditional norms—except for one child. In contrast to my siblings, I stood out as the one who did not conform, for instance, by neither covering up nor wearing the hijab. The fact that I have also been in the public eye has further magnified our differences. In our culture, people are often identified by their parents, but now my family members are identified by my name. It is both a blessing and a curse, as they sometimes receive respect and love because of my achievements. But at other times, they face disrespect and even threats because of me.

As my father ages, I want to forge stronger relationships with my mum and dad's children. My siblings are important to me, and I have deep respect for them, even if our values are different. With so many half-siblings from my father's other wives, I have found it difficult to develop relationships with them. We are talking about twenty-six other brothers and sisters. So for now I am concentrating on growing closer to my full siblings and the one half-sibling I raised like a daughter, Aisha.

I deeply love my parents and siblings, yet it has taken a long time for me to get over the feelings of abandonment and betrayal I felt when I was forced into my first marriage and then was essentially left to survive on my own in New York City as a young immigrant girl. At a time when they could have offered me compassion and comfort, all I felt was judgment and despair. The year after my divorce from Muhamed was when I lost hope.

Chapter 6

Losing Hope

WHEN I WAS SIXTEEN, I was very slim, with big breasts. Everywhere I went, the attention was on my breasts. I had escaped my first marriage, and now all the men were asking me out or sexually harassing me. Even though I was young, men saw me as a sexual object rather than a person. I did not know how to deal with it, especially right after my mother's death and my arrival in a foreign country. Whenever I was outside my home, I felt uneasy and scared.

At home, I felt the same emotions, but for different reasons. At the time, I was living in the Bronx with my aunt and uncle, grateful they had provided me with a place to stay. But it was clear that I had invaded their space and was seen as an outsider. My cousins, whom I am very close with today, did not understand why I was staying in their home. They would find me watching television and would tell me to go back to my father's house. I do not blame them for statements like that, because they were young and innocent. At one point, I snapped over their treatment of me and pushed one of my cousins, who fell and broke either his arm or leg. I do not remember which, but I remember my immense guilt. I had no intention of hurting him, but I did.

My uncle was terrific. He never judged me, and he made me feel like his home was mine. Everyone else made me feel like I was a burden and like they did not want me there—particularly my aunt. When I tried to focus on my homework, she would assign me new household chores, making it incredibly difficult for me to concentrate on my studies. She would call me lazy and make fun of me, saying no man would ever love me, since I knew nothing about household chores and cooking. For a variety of reasons, my uncle was not in a position to intercede on my behalf.

This constant pressure left me feeling frayed at the edges and perpetually stressed. I frequently found myself entangled in heated arguments with her. She never missed an opportunity to remind me of what she deemed were my shortcomings. My aunt would talk with her friends about me and say: "She is this washed-up girl who has already had sex. She is not a virgin anymore. No one wants her." I would be in the room, listening to what they said, and it hurt me deeply.

Determined to continue my education and find a safer space to study, I sought more secure employment than the odd jobs I had held so far. I found work at a restaurant, where I often stayed late into the night, after my shifts, to finish my schoolwork. That job provided stability with a salary of $1.75 an hour and tips. However, things took a dark turn when the restaurant manager began taking advantage of my situation by subjecting me to sexual assault. My reality was grim; not a single day passed without him touching, cornering, and instilling fear in me.

My options were limited as an undocumented immigrant. Speaking out seemed impossible, and I felt trapped in this situation since I could not find another job due to my status. Losing that job would mean losing my only means of survival in an unforgiving city, where I was left to fend for myself. My dad and my siblings never sent me a penny, and no one ever asked me if I needed anything.

Everyone knew this restaurant manager was a predator. Every woman who worked at that restaurant had a story about the experiences she had endured because of him. As an adult, I have felt a tremendous internal conflict about seeking justice for myself. The restaurant was established by an immigrant family living outside the United States at the time. They were unaware of what was going on. It feels like a moral dilemma, seeking justice for the harm done to me while not wanting to possibly ruin the lives of the restaurant owners, who had been kind to me.

Navigating my way through my school years was a formidable challenge. My grasp of English made communication with my peers a strenuous effort. It seemed they could not comprehend the language barrier and my intense personal battles. Every day was a relentless cycle of adversity, with difficulties at school followed by strife at home and then even more hurdles at my job. This amalgamation of persistent troubles gradually pushed me into despair, to the point where I started to lose the will to live.

Following my mother's death, I felt as if I had become nothing but a burden, and even my father seemed to have cast me aside. I perpetually felt out of place and uncared for, and I was constantly grappling with a profound loneliness and rejection. In those moments when I voiced my feelings or showed my reactions, guilt would engulf me, adding to the mounting weight of isolation and sadness that seemed to dictate my life.

I was so miserable that instead of going home at night, I would do my homework and sleep on the B and D subway trains until morning, when I went to school. There were days when I was exhausted. As soon as I boarded the train, I would fall asleep, only to wake up to the danger of the nighttime surroundings. It was far from a safe environment, and it intensified my already heightened anxiety. I was constantly on edge, jumpy at the slightest noises or even at a simple "Hey." The experience was even more unsettling because of the inappropriate remarks from men on the train. Their comments about my appearance and my body were unwarranted, made me deeply uncomfortable, and were never-ending, which added a layer of vulnerability to an already distressing situation.

Sometimes, young men who frequented the restaurant would deliberately arrive late, knowing I was responsible for closing up and would have to take the train. They would offer to drive me home, either to ensure my safety or to try to get a date with me. Each time a different man dropped me off in the Bronx, my aunt would accuse me of being involved with him. This fostered a widespread rumor in the community about my supposed relationships with these men. People began to scrutinize and judge my character based on these late-night rides home, assuming that they and I had the worst intentions. These false allegations, spread by gossip and fueled by assumptions, were profoundly hurtful and significantly impacted me. I was merely trying to get home safely after a long night at work. Still, my actions were twisted into something sinister, harming my reputation and my well-being.

I think, at some point, I became numb to my feelings. I had my anxiety; I was scared. Aside from that, I do not remember how everything affected me. I just know I wanted to die. I just wanted to be done with all of this. It is just too much. I was fighting everything. I was fighting to survive. I was fighting to get an education and, most importantly, to be who I wanted to be. The trauma had caught up with me, and having an unsupportive family made it even worse. I was at my breaking point. I was in deep trouble.

I never thought about reaching out to my father and my siblings, who were scattered all over the world. I was never the type to ask for things, and they never bothered to ask me if I needed anything. If I had told them I did not want to live anymore, they would have said I was out of my mind, rude, did not have faith, and did not believe in God. I think that is how they would have perceived my state of mind.

I vividly remember the day before I decided to kill myself. An egg hit my head, thrown by some kids from the building across from my school. It was like an open declaration of war, a daily reminder of the bullying I faced. For some reason, the incident triggered something deep inside me. The relentless issues at home, the problems at work, and now this. It just felt like too much.

The next day, my mind was a whirlpool of despair and frustration. Amid the chaos in my head, I took some pills. I cannot recall how or when the school learned what I had done. Nancy Todd, who ran the school's health clinic, called a local hospital. I refused to go, convinced they would misunderstand my struggles and deem me mentally unstable. Thankfully, the school took a different approach and contacted Taina and my Sanctuary family. When they arrived at the school, their unwavering support and care convinced me to go to the hospital for much-needed help.

The next thing I remember was ending up in a Manhattan hospital. The experience felt surreal. I felt trapped, surrounded by people I perceived as "crazy." Initially, I felt furious about being confined to a lockdown ward, with no freedom to move around. As the days passed, a strange kind of peace settled over me. The hospital became a haven from work, school, and family drama. I realized the doctors genuinely wanted to help me and did not see me as crazy. Taina remained a constant presence throughout my stay, visiting me every day. She brought me books, such as *I Know Why the Caged Bird Sings*, believing they would aid my healing process. She also encouraged me to keep a journal, something to help me express my thoughts and emotions.

Even during my hospitalization, the troubles with my family persisted. While I agreed to see my uncle during a visit, I refused to see my aunt due to her hurtful actions. Unfortunately, she retaliated by spreading a damaging rumor in our community, claiming I was getting an abortion. Despite my anger at this, I resolved not to let it affect me and chose to focus on the love and support from my found family.

This was my first exposure to mental health counseling and prescription medication. That stint lasted about two weeks, and then I found myself back at my aunt and uncle's place, the environment that had contributed to my mental state. It was not my choice to live there; it was a lack of what I perceived as options that landed me there. Taina had always opened her doors for me, but moving in with her felt like a permanent separation from my family, a step I was not ready to take. I feared losing the only family I had ever known.

Back at my aunt and uncle's place, the environment was

suffocating. The whispers, gossip, and lack of privacy were relentless. My aunt would listen in on my calls, an invasive presence constantly hovering over me. It felt like I was living in a fishbowl, my every move scrutinized, every word analyzed. The negativity permeated every aspect of that house, even influencing my little cousins' perception of me. I was labeled, burdened by the rumors and whispers, which seemed to cling to the walls of that place.

Fortunately, Nancy, who had helped me so much during my suicide attempt, became a vital support at school. She became a significant part of my life and extended her care until I graduated in June 2007. She even attended my graduation ceremony. School gradually got better. I finally had the chance to experience being a regular teenager again. It had been a long time since I felt this sense of normalcy, and I relished every moment. Participating in teen activities, prom, and celebrating my graduation with friends at the restaurant where I worked brought me happiness. But the tiny bit of happiness was gone when I no longer had school.

Home and work remained constant sources of pain. There was little support from family or friends. I was so tired. I knew if I did not escape New York City, all the bad things would happen again. I faced what seemed to be three choices. I could return to the Gambia, where I feared encountering the same difficulties, enter into a second arranged marriage in the United States, or end my life. I was only seventeen, and the complexities of my life were absolutely overwhelming.

A part of me clung desperately to my family, as they were all I knew. My anxiety amplified my fears about my family, constantly making me worry about the repercussions of losing them. Anxiety, compounded with the derogatory labels and perceptions imposed upon me, began to mold my view of myself, unfortunately reinforcing a negative self-image. This distorted perception influenced many of the issues I encountered later in my life. I became mired in self-doubt, never fully convinced that I was worthy of love or that someone could genuinely care for me. I felt perpetually seen as a burden, which ingrained in me an overwhelming feeling of worthlessness.

I knew if I ended my life, I would go to hell. That was what my religion had always taught me. But I already felt I was in hell on earth. I felt abandoned by God. My faith had left me. I was ready to surrender in whatever way I could to end the pain and the loneliness.

Chapter 7

Surrender and Perseverance

Y COUSIN FATOUMATA, who is related to me on my mother's side, visited New York. Upon hearing the swirl of rumors and the disparaging remarks being circulated about me, she felt a deep concern for my well-being. She did not just sit back and watch events unfold; she took a proactive role in trying to safeguard me. She firmly believed it was essential for me to break away from the situation fostering all this negativity. So she arranged to have a sincere, heart-to-heart talk with me in order to share her perspective on the matter.

During our conversation, Fatoumata expressed her distress and suggested her husband facilitate a marriage between his brother and me to provide me a fresh start. This way I could leave behind the adverse circumstances engulfing me and step into a life unmarred by baseless talk and rumors. She emphasized that taking this step was vital for me, not only to protect my personal dignity but also to preserve the good name of my late mother, who was well respected in the community. She implored me to speak with my father, explain the gravity of the situation, and urged him to support my decision to get married.

I realized that following through with her suggestion might be my only escape and gathered the courage to call my father. Looking back, I understand this call was not a plea for help but a decisive step toward reclaiming control over my life. I chose marriage as a way of taking care of myself. I was done fighting and was very tired. My spirit had taken a beating.

My best friend, Haddy, felt like this second marriage was rushed. She also thought I was still traumatized. She did not want me to go through with it, but I wanted to leave New York and everything that had occurred there. I was also afraid to return to the Gambia. There I would have no Taina, no Sanctuary, and no laws to protect me. So when I met Hajie, I decided to give marriage a chance. He was just ten years older than me, seemed more open to my ideas, and was not focused on controlling me.

You may wonder how a rebel like me consented to a second marriage as a child bride. I can only say I was numb inside, a feeling that would stay with me until the birth of my daughter. I had spent so much of my life caught between what I believed and what my religion and culture wanted me to think. I had grown tired of feeling like I was always on the outside. I wanted the comfort and protection of family.

Surprisingly, Hajie and I got along well. I felt okay about him, and with relief, I agreed to marry him in September 2007 and move to Atlanta. However, Hajie had a first wife and a son, so I became a second wife. They lived in the Gambia, which meant I did not have to live with them. I had always told my mother I would never be a second wife to anyone. Yet at this point, I did not care. All I wanted was to get out of New York.

I tried my best to ignore the existence of his first wife, but it became increasingly difficult since Hajie kept in contact with her. The situation became even more challenging when his mother insisted he bring her and his son to the United States to live with us. I vehemently refused to share my husband with another woman. Hajie assured me he would not bring her over, professed his love for me, and claimed his first marriage had been forced upon him. Although I had doubts about the future, especially considering Hajie's tendency to do whatever his mother wanted, I believed him.

As the months went by, I got used to the situation with Hajie and believed he cared for me. I cared for him. However, our marriage was marred by the challenging experience of three miscarriages, a common side effect of FGM. It took a toll on both of us. Nevertheless, I carried my fourth pregnancy to full term and was filled with immense joy. Unfortunately, Hajie refused to accompany me to doctors' appointments, which hurt and frustrated me. When I went into labor, he drove me to the hospital and promptly left. Eventually, he came to the hospital after receiving the news he had a son. He allowed his mother to name our child Muhammad without consulting me. I do not think his actions meant he was intentionally a bad person, but I do believe he lacked comprehension and emotional intelligence. During those moments, I thought Hajie did not love me or care about my feelings, but I have come to realize that he is the kind of person who just does not get it.

After giving birth, I drove myself back home, a pattern that would repeat itself with the birth of my daughter, Khadija, and my youngest son, Abu. Becoming a mother at a young age brought about a multitude of emotions. The joy and excitement of having children were undeniable, but there was an underlying reality I could not escape. The more children I bore for my husband, the stronger the possibility I would become trapped in a marriage.

Our relationship started to decline after the birth of our first child in 2009, due to the stress a newborn brings to a couple's life and my realization that Hajie and I had very little in common. My husband was not intellectually inclined, and I loved learning. He would change the television channel to his preference even when I was watching something, so I would retreat to my room to focus on my books. If I expressed a desire to go to a restaurant, he would view it as me trying to be someone I was not. When I mentioned going on vacation, he would dismiss it with laughter. He often criticized aspects of my life, from my clothing choices to my friends. He regularly complained to my family, making me feel like my individuality and essence were under constant scrutiny. While these may seem like little things, they added up to an unhappy home in which I made all the compromises.

One night, Hajie attempted to leave the house during an

argument, and I stood in his way. He then informed me he would bring his first wife to the United States if I could not be obedient. I threatened to leave him if he did so, and he coldly told me I was free to do as I wished. However, lacking the financial means to support myself and my son, I had no choice but to stay. I tried communicating my unhappiness to my family, hoping for their understanding and support. However, they urged me to persevere, emphasizing the well-being of my children and suggesting love was not essential in a marriage. Given my personality and aspirations, it was difficult for me to understand how my family expected me to find happiness.

I knew it was time to fight for my independence when Hajie made it clear he intended to bring his son and first wife, who was also his first cousin, to Atlanta. I knew I did not want to stay in a house with a co-wife. I knew education was my only way out if I decided to leave. I enrolled in a community college, opting for it based on its affordability. I was determined to obtain a degree that would lead to a well-paying job, which would allow me to support myself and my children. As I worked through college, juggling nursing my son, giving birth to two more children, and enduring the pain of sharing my husband with another woman, I promised myself my anguish would all end the day I graduated and secured better employment.

Hajie's marriage to his first wife ended before I gave birth to my youngest son, Abu. I became his only wife, but by then, I had already left the marriage emotionally. Intensely unhappy, I knew I did not want to stay in the marriage. Being in the marriage was suffocating me, and sharing a bed with my husband had become too hard. I did not want my children to live in the turmoil I had experienced because of the relationship between my father and my mum.

I will say that Hajie was a very supportive father and loved his children deeply. I worked many hours and was always in school, so he helped take care of the children when they were young. He did things that men in our community did not do traditionally. He would bathe the kids, help me take them to day care, and sometimes cook. These were things I truly appreciated about him, and they are why to this day I still harbor some guilt for walking away. But he could also be very traditional and rigid, and I did not want my children to be constantly exposed to his views of men's and women's roles. I was already seeing the impact of these beliefs on my sons and daughter, and I felt it would limit their opportunities and happiness in the future.

I became more involved in my Atlanta community, particularly by helping immigrant women and girls, a good number of whom had been affected by FGM and child marriages. Many were uneducated and experiencing economic hardship. One of my reasons for helping was that I could not stand by and refrain from lending a hand to ease the pain. Another was that aiding others was an escape from my own unhappiness.

I did this secretly to keep an uneasy peace in my home. As long as my husband was kept unaware of what I was doing, we lived with our situation. However, later, when my actions became public, our relationship took a turn for the worse. I became the source of gossip. People kept asking him why he was letting me do what I was doing. He would come home angry most of the time, and I had to endure being told almost on a daily basis that I was going to hell.

I wanted to be let out of the marriage. When I speak of "being let out" of an arranged marriage, I mean receiving my family's blessing, especially my father's, to end it. His opinion has always been paramount in my life. I have consistently made choices to make him proud, and his expectations heavily influenced my marriage decisions. My husband recognized this family dynamic and thought I would never leave without my family's approval. Our emotional distance grew, and we even stopped sharing a bed.

My siblings seemed more understanding, hinting that they would rather support my decisions than see me unhappy. However, my father reminded me of my past choices, implying the failures were on me. After ending my first marriage, I had sworn to my father I would commit to my second one. Little did I know that this promise would take a toll on me, killing a part of who I was. So, I lived as the picture-perfect wife for nearly a decade, diligently cooking and caring for my home and children. Despite my efforts to suppress it, a spark within me refused to die. People could still sense a wildness in me, though I kept much of it hidden, immersing myself in education and work.

Looking back, I realize that my need for the approval of my family and community pushed me into this marriage. I felt compelled to marry as a means of gaining their acceptance. Yet I now recognize I did not allow myself to recover from the trauma in New York City or allow myself time to get to know Hajie before I agreed to the marriage. Working, getting my education, and hearing the stories of other women made me realize the importance of freedom and choice. I did not need to compromise myself to meet other people's expectations. I could become an activist, not only for others but also in my own life.

ACTIVIST

To me, an activist is not just someone who rallies against the oppressive forces of the world; she or he is someone who, in the face of injustice, chooses selflessness over selfishness, putting others' needs before personal desires.

Activism is a choice. A conscious decision to stand on the right side of history, advocating for the marginalized, the misunderstood, and the disenfranchised. It is about believing in the inherent equality we all share, seeing all human beings in the same light, and making the arduous choice between right and wrong.

An activist's journey is about more than just roaring against the wind. It is about the silent moments, the pauses where one leans in to listen. There is humility to true activism, an understanding that every voice has a story.

Chapter 8

A Daughter Inspires

WHEN I WAS PREGNANT WITH my second child, the ultra-sound revealed I was having a daughter. I had prayed to have only sons since I feared the challenges and struggles a daughter might face. Raising a child who could potentially go through hardships similar to those I had experienced was something I wanted to avoid. Having a daughter was never my intention, and if I had had a choice, I would not have chosen to have one—or so I thought.

Seeing that ultrasound was a turning point. Yes, I started feeling anxiety while contemplating the life she might lead. I harbored a fear of being unable to shield her from the cultural norms and traditions that could potentially harm her. I worried she might have the same personality as me and fretted about how my family and society might view her. I had always felt like a problem within my family, a burden simply by being me.

However, I soon realized God had been very good to me and had fulfilled a dream I did not even know I carried: to have a precious daughter and name her Khadija. The name Khadija, meaning "trustworthy and respectful" in Arabic, holds deep significance. It is the name of the Prophet Muhammad's first wife and the mother of his children. The Qur'an describes her as one of the four perfect women. Both my husbands have mothers named Khadija, reaffirming my belief that faith and destiny intertwine in mysterious ways. Coincidences? I do not believe in them.

At Atlanta Medical Center, I gave birth to Khadija on March 17, 2010. Due to my petite frame and the size of my baby, my doctor induced labor a few days after my due date. During that delivery and the others, I was torn as my body struggled to stretch as much as was required. The scar tissue from FGM made the necessary expansion nearly impossible, and as a result, tearing became a recurring issue. Just as it had with my painful miscarriages, FGM continued to impact my life.

Khadija entered the world, a beautiful baby girl who bore a striking resemblance to me, with chubby cheeks that mirrored my own in infancy. But there was one significant difference. If we had been in the Gambia, my daughter would have been subjected to female genital mutilation within a week of her birth. That would never happen to her.

Khadija gave me a sense of purpose. She was a divine gift from God. I gazed into her eyes and recognized everything I had done and would continue to do was worth it. I understood protecting my precious girl would be a tremendous responsibility. My world would revolve around ensuring she lived the life I was unjustly denied. I was prepared to do whatever it took to protect her.

My bond with my daughter transcends anything I have experienced before. As a parent, I see similar traits in her. She is intuitive, sensitive, and responsible, just like me. It warms my heart to see her caring nature, but at the same time, I do not want her to carry the same burden I do. I want her to grow up without feeling responsible for my happiness or anyone else's. I am determined to raise her differently from how my mother raised me by being mindful of my words and actions, ensuring they never inflict lasting pain on Khadija or her brothers. With its emphasis on open communication and an absence of force and violence, my parenting approach has thus far proven successful.

My children are the embodiment of a mother's pride. My oldest, Muhammad, is fourteen, and he has such a clean heart. While he looks like his father, he has a very different personality than him. He does not keep anger inside him. Within ten minutes, he forgives and is on to something else, like playing soccer, which he loves so much. He sees everyone in the world as good, a quality I both admire and am fearful of for him. When he was younger, I also worried he would incorporate the more traditional views of his father about girls and boys. I remember him telling his sister she could not do something, because she was a girl. Recently, he came to me with the idea that we should buy a large plot of land and build houses on it for child brides who cannot escape their husbands. He knows my story, honors it, and wants to make things better for women who are trapped, often because they lack money to get out of their situation.

Abu is a mini-me. My youngest son and the other children are getting a high-quality classic education that also incorporates Islamic studies. At age nine, Abu exhibits the same curiosity and intelligence I had when I went to school in the Gambia. Like me, he is also a mischief-maker. He loves to dance and has a passion for basketball. While I wanted to be the president of the Gambia when I was his age, he wants to be a star player for the NBA. We both like to dream big.

At thirteen, Khadija possesses an awareness of self and a remarkable ability to impact the world with her intelligence and kindness. She is, without a doubt, the smartest and kindest little girl I have ever known, brimming with a genuine and compassionate heart. Some might say I am overprotective of my daughter. I do not think so. I know what men can do to a young girl child.

When I was growing up, it was customary for multiple family members to live with us; some were not good people. I have already shared my story about being abused by members of our household. I was on guard to make sure it did not happen. In the African communities in Atlanta, people often live with their brothers, wives, and extended families in big houses. When my husband proposed that his brothers come live with us to help with rent, I refused and told him I preferred to work for the money. It was not because I believed they were pedophiles, but because so many bad things happened to me as a child. Because of my past, I did not want to live with anyone except my husband and children. My concerns also extended to social events. I would not let my husband take Khadija with him to places where men were around. Essentially, she was always with me.

As I engaged with other families and shared my concerns, I discovered the problem was more pervasive than I had initially grasped. Some resorted to making tasteless jokes about subjecting Khadija to FGM to silence me. At the same time, grown men even jested about her becoming their wife. In our culture, such jokes are disturbingly familiar. Still, given my own painful experiences during childhood, I could never condone or tolerate them. I engaged in countless arguments, only for people to downplay their remarks as humor. During these exchanges, they branded me as difficult and incapable of taking a joke.

I never anticipated that my activism would extend beyond fighting for Khadija to advocating within our immediate Gambian community in Atlanta. Observing Khadija grow older and witnessing her unwavering spirit ignited a fire within me. With a group of volunteers, I initiated training programs for doctors in the Atlanta area, enlightening them about the importance of providing culturally sensitive care to women who have experienced FGM. Furthermore, when daughters were born, we ensured there were resources at the hospital to educate parents about the detrimental effects of such practices. Over the years, we successfully trained more than one thousand doctors across the United States, arming them with the tools to serve these women better.

When Khadija reached the age when she would soon enter the school system, potentially alongside other African students, it became imperative to me to ensure that schools developed an understanding of these harmful practices and treated girls from African communities with empathy. Consequently, we organized seminars and training sessions for educators and counselors to enlighten them about the issues facing girls and foster cultural sensitivity. This effort yielded remarkable results, as many teachers had never encountered FGM and were shocked by its existence. The revelations opened avenues for dialogue and cooperation as the teachers began to comprehend the importance of collective action and support.

I realized I had the power to amplify the voices of countless Khadijas worldwide. Every action I took through my activism against FGM and child marriage was aimed to equip parents facing circumstances similar to mine with the knowledge and resources necessary to shield their daughters from these harmful traditional practices. As I raise my daughter, it is against a backdrop of what happened to me and what I experience today in the world around me.

I am often confronted with a harsh reality during visits to my home country. Driving through the Gambia, I witness young girls who should be in school running through the streets, balancing plates on their heads to contribute to their families' livelihoods. Thankfully, my daughter's future does not mirror theirs. I made a deliberate choice, deviating from the path of cultural expectations. As I observe these girls, I am acutely aware many will be thrust into unwanted circumstances simply because they lack the freedom to choose. The theme of choice intertwines with poverty, leaving me firmly convinced that empowering girls from a young age through direct investment is the only path toward equality and equity.

Child marriage represents planned poverty—a cruel fate, one I vehemently oppose for Khadija. My initial motivation to advocate for girls stemmed from the desire to protect my daughter, but that aspiration quickly expanded beyond personal boundaries. The magnitude of the challenges facing girls struck me deeply. Millions of girls worldwide have endured the torment of forced marriage, and women carry the lifelong burden of FGM. It became clear that defending my daughter and amplifying her voice were not enough when countless other girls suffered and perished silently. This suffering transcends the confines of a single community; it should evoke outrage, particularly among parents blessed with daughters.

Khadija forever holds a special place in my heart. Her life contrasts starkly with my own upbringing. When I was her age, I was trapped in an impending arranged marriage. In contrast, Khadija has to contend only with the challenges of being a girl in a world that offers her the freedom to soar. She has been my guiding light and a constant inspiration throughout my journey. Her unwavering support and personal growth have fueled my passion for empowering daughters worldwide. She has become a compassionate and resilient young woman. When I embarked on this journey of advocating for the rights of daughters worldwide, she stood by my side, providing unwavering support and encouragement. I suspect she will always be one of my fiercest protectors.

Every story has a beginning. Inspired by my daughter, I started small by performing acts that directly helped women and girls in the Atlanta community. I became a behind-the-scenes "underground activist," planting the seeds that would later take me into vigorous advocacy in the Gambia and beyond.

Chapter 9

The Underground Activist

ATLANTA WAS HOME TO A vibrant community of immigrant families from both West and East Africa during the time I was there, from 2007 to 2017. Even today, it ranks behind only New York City, Miami, and Washington, D.C., as the city with the largest foreign-born Black population. I was most familiar with the Gambian community in Atlanta; our lives were intertwined, and everyone seemed to know everyone else's business. Most of our husbands worked in the bustling flea market, each with a stall where they sold various items. The women gathered for community engagements, while our children attended the mosque to learn the Qur'an and deepen their understanding of Islam, just as we had done when we were young.

Across the United States, immigrant communities often have civil society organizations catering to their needs. However, the Gambian community in Atlanta primarily relied on the mosques, a tradition that continues today. Most of our children were young, and few women were educated. Although there was no one I could confide in about my feelings or ambitions, I was curious about the women I met at the mosque and various community events, like weddings and naming ceremonies. Were their past and current experiences similar to mine? I knew what I lived with and how the silence killed me inside. I wanted to see if I was alone on this journey, and I quickly realized I was not.

When I started my work, I saw it not as activism but as an outlet. Back then, I loved cooking and hosting people at my home, and at these hosting events, young women would gather, sometimes bringing food they had prepared. We would talk about our marriages and the similar issues we were facing. We would spend our evening together until it was time for the husbands to return from work and pick everyone up.

During these intimate moments, I witnessed the hidden suffering the women endured. They would put on smiles and sing praises about their husbands in public. However, they shared stories of violence and unhappiness in our private conversations. It broke my heart. I focused on listening, but not everyone saw it this way. Being a mother with a daughter changed many things for me. I could not stay silent. I could not be passive. I became deeply affected by listening to the women's stories and witnessing their trauma. I felt compelled to provide advice, share my experiences, and connect them to available resources and opportunities. Some husbands complained about me and claimed I was corrupting their wives. Some even went as far as telling their wives not to hang out with me.

Every morning I would wake up with a heavy burden, knowing the challenges women and girls in my community faced. I would spend hours searching for resources to assist them. I aided families with asylum and human-trafficking issues, often seeking pro bono lawyers to take their cases. Through this work, I crossed paths with Monica Khant, the executive director of Georgia Asylum and Immigration Network (GAIN), who provided invaluable support and collaboration. Over time, I became a trusted resource for women and girls in our community, addressing the various problems they faced. Back then, I did not fully comprehend the impact of my work. It is only now, as I reconnect with the families I assisted and hear how their lives have changed, that I realize the profound significance of helping one person at a time.

When I started working with these communities, I focused mainly on the West African population, particularly girls from the Gambia. It saddened me to witness these girls' struggles, including being subjected to FGM and pressured into early marriages. Many believed these practices were normal, until they were trapped in marriages they could not escape. Many women in our community transitioned from apartments to houses, thanks to their husbands buying homes and SUVs. I lacked those luxuries, so I partnered with Atlanta Habitat for Humanity and proudly built my first home. It was not my dream house, but it gave me a sense of belonging.

With my newfound construction knowledge, I helped single mothers and widows in our community access affordable housing. I assisted them throughout the application process and volunteered to help build their homes. I love building houses and would consider construction as a hobby if I ever have free time. When I retire, I would like to be just like President Jimmy Carter, one of my personal heroes. I can imagine starting a program like Habitat for Humanity in the Gambia, where I can help women build homes.

There were days when I received distress calls from women trapped in their houses, unable to leave for weeks. I would drive to their homes and find ways to unlock their garages, enabling them to go to the store and get the necessities they needed. I acquired handyman skills by building my home and became proficient in such tasks as breaking into garages. I suspect Habitat for Humanity never thought their training would be used that way.

One of my significant accomplishments involved starting an after-school program in Clarkston, Georgia, site of the state's largest immigrant and refugee community. Refugees from Ethiopia, Somalia, Eritrea, Sudan, Congo, and other African countries belonged to this community. Many families in Clarkston lived in severe poverty and had not integrated into mainstream American society. They did not know the opportunities that were available to them. To better understand their living conditions, I initiated a door-to-door campaign to identify the children and gain deeper insights into their circumstances. Initially, twenty participants joined the after-school program, but it gradually grew.

The program was not limited to girls; boys also joined. My group of volunteers created a safe space for the children to discuss their home and school challenges, provided homework support, and introduced extracurricular activities, like yoga and financial literacy. We aided parents in navigating WIC (the Special Supplemental Nutrition Program for Women, Infants, and Children), completing food stamp applications, and exploring other available community resources.

Mam Harr Gaye assisted me with this program and was one of the best people I ever hired. She connected with the children in our program, and they all called her Aunty Mam Harr. She was so invested in their success, and I watched us both grow through our interactions with program participants. Mam Harr became the program manager for Safe Hands for Girls, the nonprofit I founded to help with these efforts and which I will talk about in-depth later in this book.

I also continued to address the issues closest to my heart. One young woman named Fatima was being sent to Mali to undergo FGM. When I learned about it, I was deeply concerned and spent significant time with her parents, pleading with them not to subject Fatima to the procedure. I assured Fatima's parents that I would take responsibility for providing her with sex education and emphasizing the value of a good education. I firmly believed that giving Fatima a chance to understand and embrace these concepts was essential. Her parents agreed not to subject Fatima to FGM. Eventually, I took on the role of a mentor to her parents to help address their worries about what they saw as negative American behaviors, such as engaging in sexual activities and becoming pregnant outside of marriage.

When two girls in our after-school program got pregnant, we knew it was important to start a sexual education program for our girls and boys. This was a very challenging topic because of the culture of silence about sex in the community. Because some of our girls were sexually active, we wanted to provide them with necessary information on topics such as contraceptives. We were worried about the parents' reactions, so we trod very carefully in order not to risk their removing their children from the program. Eventually, we built a certain amount of trust with the parents. Mam Harr did a very good job of running this program; she had a better balance of spirituality and cultural sensitivity than me at that point and was incredibly smart.

It was important that I showed these immigrant families my African identity in order to demonstrate my dedication and bridge the cultural gap. I chose not to wear Western clothes in their presence, instead embracing African attire and adorning my head. This helped them see I remained rooted in African values and traditions, despite being educated. Becoming a role model for these girls became my responsibility, and I was careful not to engage in any actions that would validate the parents' concerns. They needed to see I genuinely cared for their children's well-being and was committed to helping them build a better future.

I formed a powerful bond with the older children in my program. They saw me as a second mother, despite the closeness in our ages. Everyone called me Aunty Jaha, and they eagerly looked forward to our after-school activities. We taught them about financial planning, helped them create résumés, and assisted with internship applications and financial aid opportunities. While this work brought an immense sense of fulfillment, hearing about the children's hardships and helping them navigate life's challenges consumed my thoughts and sometimes left me sleepless at night.

To help them, I became an entrepreneur and learned how to sew and sell clothes to bridge the gaps left by state resources. My full-time job as a personal banker at Wells Fargo Bank made me a valuable resource for many people. My relationship with the Gambian community improved significantly when I helped many of the husbands who worked in the flea markets open bank accounts, something they had never done before in the United States. Additionally, I started educating them about financial literacy and the importance of building their credit. Not one to sit behind my desk at the bank, I convinced my manager, Debra Myers, to let me meet potential clients at discount malls and flea markets. This was a very successful strategy, as it inspired many immigrants to open accounts. I suspect that if I had stayed with Wells Fargo, I would have gone far at the bank.

Looking back, I cannot fully comprehend how I juggled everything while attending school, working, and being a wife and a mother. But it was worth it and gave me hope, especially when I witnessed the children in my program graduate, excel academically, and gain admission to college. Initially, they never believed college was within their reach, but they proved themselves wrong through their determination and talent. While I am grateful for the messages of gratitude they send, I do not need reminders of how we helped. Their success speaks for itself.

My husband knew little about my activities outside the house, and so did my family. Keeping this work a secret was one of the most challenging aspects of my life at the time. It caused me considerable anxiety, as I felt I had a split personality. He assumed I was working and then returning home. I ensured everything was in order when he returned by cooking and keeping the house clean. I never viewed my actions as extraordinary or unusual at the time; I believed it was something we should all do for others. However, balancing the roles of dutiful wife at home and "secret" community advocate took its toll on my mental health.

I engaged in a careful balance between my activism and the need to protect my husband and family from potential judgment, because I despised the thought of my actions causing trouble for my loved ones. They were ill equipped to handle the criticism I often faced. Still, my work breathed life into me, instilling hope and a sense of purpose. It allowed me to connect with new people and make a positive impact, regardless of whether anyone recognized or praised my efforts. My concern lay solely with the harsh criticism from those who would never understand why my actions were so necessary.

What was particularly painful was the judgment from my family. My sister Fatoumata, who also lived in Atlanta, had grown up with me. However, our personalities were vastly different. Fatoumata was considered the quiet, beautiful, religious, and pious sister, while

I had been labeled the opposite. At times, it seemed like my sister was embarrassed by me, especially in public. This hurt me deeply, and I blamed myself for not being as perfect or as pretty as she was. It felt as though everyone adored her, while I was the black sheep. Despite the hurt, I could not blame my sister entirely, as people often said negative things about me, portraying me as a bad person due to my outspoken nature and refusal to tolerate disrespect.

At home, my marriage continued to fail. As I have mentioned, my father held great significance in my life, particularly after my mum's death. My promise to him that I would protect my marriage and shield our community from further ridicule was paramount to me. Yet try as I might, I could never truly achieve this. There was always something I did or some flaw in my approach. Consequently, I kept my home life and my activism separate. This strategy worked for me. I resided in Atlanta but worked with the refugee population in Clarkston, and this physical distance allowed my activism to flourish without public outrage. As I look back, these were undoubtedly the best days of my journey as an activist. However, the challenge lay in keeping most of my activities hidden.

Thankfully, I had the unwavering support of my best friend, Haddy. She understood my struggles better than anyone and provided a safe space for me to share. Though she lived in Maryland, she would visit frequently and was the sole confidant who knew I was unhappy with my marriage. Remarkably, she never judged, humorously asking me each night, "What problems did you cause today?"

In hindsight, I realized the challenges and predicaments I faced living a double life left my husband feeling bewildered. It was such a frightening time in many ways. I would travel outside of Atlanta for conferences or seminars, only to miss my flights and succumb to anxiety attacks. I would call Haddy in tears, because I feared my husband and did not want our home transformed into a war zone. I knew better than to provoke him on those occasions. I alleviated tensions at home by assisting my husband with bills and taking care of other responsibilities, hoping it would soften his frustrations with me. I constantly invented excuses for my whereabouts and late arrivals. When I reached home before him, I felt relieved, as this eliminated the need for explanations about my activities. However, if I was ever late for any reason, fear and paranoia consumed me.

Sometimes I wonder where I got the ability to live a dual life. It partially stems from my childhood, where there was a stark disparity between my dreams and the reality that enveloped me. I swiftly learned to adapt accordingly in every circumstance. I adopted two distinct personas, which were both me. Within the confines of my childhood home, I assumed the role of the dutiful daughter my parents desired. Once I ventured beyond those walls, I became the individual known as Jaha, who embodied my true aspirations.

But the primary reason why I was able to live this life was that the work itself gave me immense joy. Every individual I could help became a victory. Through my "underground" work, I built strong relationships with the women I supported. Today many of them have graduated from college, secured jobs, and made positive contributions in various fields. While I am not in touch with most of them, I cherish the time I spent working with them. The sense of fulfillment I felt was immeasurable.

In Georgia I had the privilege of working with incredible children who had experienced the hardships of refugee life. As I ventured into different communities, I encountered young girls and boys hailing from war-torn countries, such as Eritrea, Sudan, Ethiopia, and Congo, and they became like a second family to me. They left an indelible mark on my soul, and even today they reach out to me through social media. I witnessed their incredible transformation. Their stories of success and happiness remind me of the profound influence we can all have when we expose young minds to new possibilities.

I remember a young man named Kofi contacting me on social media when he graduated from college. He expressed his gratitude, telling me I had shown him there was a better life out there. Knowing I was part of his journey toward a better life filled me with immeasurable joy. Stories like Kofi's affirm the transformative power of the work done by all of us volunteers, showing that even a single encounter can shape the outlook and trajectory of a young life. One of the girls who touched my heart profoundly is Bana. When I first met her, her family was trapped in extreme poverty. Witnessing her transformation was nothing short of awe-inspiring. She persevered, graduated, and became a model. Today, as I look at her, I see the epitome of beauty, not only in her appearance but also in the resilience and strength she embodies. Bana's journey reminds me that our efforts are not in vain—the seeds of hope we sow can blossom into extraordinary lives.

I encountered two other girls whose stories moved me so completely. Their paths crossed mine under different circumstances. These girls were victims of trafficking: they were forcibly brought to the United States. Overwhelmed with gratitude, their mother tearfully recounted later how our efforts facilitated the girls' escape and led to their reunion. Thanks to our intervention, these girls now have their papers, citizenship, and the opportunity to pursue their dreams freely, unburdened by forced marriages or exploitation. Their story speaks to the power of a single act of kindness to forever alter the course of lives and restore hope where it had been stolen. Hearing their mother's gratitude reminded me that even when we do not fully realize the extent of our actions, we can change someone's life for the better.

These experiences led me to start a blog in which I openly discussed the challenges women faced and the societal expectation for them to remain silent and endure their pain. I also participated in online conversations on platforms like Facebook, discussing domestic violence, child marriage, and FGM. Despite my fear of judgment from my family, I never held back when expressing my opinions. In truth, I had no idea what would happen when I went from being an underground activist to a public figure in 2014.

Chapter 10

Going Public

EVEN THOUGH I WAS AN INTELLIGENT, educated woman who had traveled to three continents, was raising three children, and had been married twice, I was still, in many ways, a naive young woman. Yes, I had come a long way from my village in the Gambia, but I did not understand the hate and power that can drive this world.

I still did not define myself as an activist. I did not see what I was doing as being engaged in a war, or even a battle, against FGM and child marriage. Instead, I saw myself more like a member of the underground, fighting one-on-one to help women and young girls who needed an advocate. Like a guerilla warrior, I stayed in the background as much as I could and maintained my dual life, my very secret existence.

Little did I know my actions were about to change the course of my life. It all began with a few anonymous interviews for articles, where my name was replaced with an alias and asterisk to protect my safety. One significant interview was with *ABC World News*, where I talked about and exposed the issues. My face was hidden; however, people recognized me, which led to a backlash within my community. I was accused of being paid to expose my community's secrets and get people in trouble. Many did not understand you do not get paid for interviews.

I felt like public enemy number one and constantly tried to explain my intentions and genuine concern for what was happening to the girls and women. It was disheartening that many did not understand my motivations. Most of my family members were very angry with me because people were scared, since many members of our community were battling immigration issues. They felt that speaking out against FGM put the community at risk of more judgment and harassment. Young people worried about how their friends would perceive them. Their concerns were valid. I felt guilty and unsure about how to make it right, but I knew what I was doing was important. I could not be silent. I needed to scream to the world. With two hundred million women and girls around the world including the United States affected by FGM, people needed to realize this was not a distant problem but rather something that was happening in their backyard.

My sister Fatoumata distanced herself from me, aligning with those who did not support my cause. Seeing her side with people who spread negativity about her own sister pained me. Despite the strain in our relationship, I loved her deeply and admired her ability to find contentment as a wife. I am one of those people who does not allow negativity in my life, and I choose to embrace love. That is part of my nature. Some people find it difficult to understand, and to be honest, I am not sure why I am this way. I just know I am, and it is a quality that has gotten me through hard times.

Meanwhile, I fought against the injustices, hoping to protect others from experiencing what I had endured. My actions increased the strain on my relationship with my husband. People questioned why he allowed me to do what I was doing, which led to constant arguments at home. The rumors and gossip surrounding me made life rough, and I had to endure being constantly told I was going to hell. The isolation was intense, but what hurt even more was the fact that people questioned my motives. They thought I was doing this only for myself. This was probably the loneliest period of my life.

Although I was perceived as charismatic, strong, and brave, few realized my vulnerability. When I was alone, I would cry for hours. I wanted to explain myself but felt nothing I said made sense to them. I would always be at fault. Despite these internal struggles, my determination to spare children from the pain I experienced kept me going. I could not leave them unprotected, so I pressed forward. The more my community alienated me, the more I was motivated to be courageous and to speak my truth. In a way, the community pushed me into going public by how it treated me when it came out I was the one doing the blogs and interviews about the consequences of FGM.

At the same time this was happening to me, stories from FGM activists in the United Kingdom started appearing online. I read an inspiring account by Nimco Ali, a British social activist of Somali heritage, of her experiences. I examined a petition by a young girl named Fahma Mohamed in which she called on the UK government to allow FGM to be taught about in schools. These were Muslim girls with backgrounds similar to mine, proudly wearing the hijab and talking from their hearts. They were putting a human voice and face to the issue. For the first time, I saw survivors publicly facing a problem that had kept Muslim girls and women trapped and silent.

For us survivors who speak out, it has never been about the acclaim. We talk about very personal matters that make us uncomfortable. Yet it is necessary in order to change laws, educate more people, and build awareness about the plight of young girls and women. It is necessary to be able to create the support for nonprofits like Safe Hands for Girls, the organization I founded, which was turning into an effective and powerful force for change.

Inspired by the UK petition, I launched one of my own on Change.org, asking the Obama administration to look into the issue of FGM in the United States and determine the number of girls and women impacted. I created the petition at home with the help of a few people who had experience in activism, especially Taina and the other staff members at Equality Now. When I launched the petition, I had no expectations.

I was shocked by the response. The petition gained momentum with support from celebrities like Ashley Judd and Mia Farrow. *The*

Guardian newspaper interviewed me, shedding light on my personal story and the petition. This publicity drew even more criticism from my community, who saw it as a violation of what they believed in. Furthermore, women and men from the Gambia do not talk about sexual matters or parts of the body. They don't go public about issues. My people believe personal and family matters should always stay within the family. They were highly embarrassed by me.

People blamed my father and questioned his ability as a religious leader to guide me. They held me responsible for potentially jeopardizing asylum opportunities for FGM survivors. That did not happen, and it has never happened because of my work. In fact, bringing the issue to the forefront actually bolstered asylum opportunities. We helped more people because we were experts, supporters, and were able to find more legal help. My detractors did not know that even before I went public, I had supported behind closed doors numerous families in their immigration cases.

While hurtful, the criticism did not matter. The petition's success—it received over 220,000 signatures—led the Obama administration to order a study of FGM by the Centers for Disease Control and Prevention (CDC). At the time of the petition, nobody knew how many people in the United States were living with FGM. There was denial that it was even practiced here. Getting the data from the CDC spurred funding to support programs to eradicate FGM, because now it was clear this issue existed in the United States and the health of women and girls was threatened.

It was a significant win for me and for everyone who supported the cause. My activism gained further recognition when the *Washington Post*, *Cosmopolitan*, ABC News, CNN, the BBC, and Al Jazeera covered my story. As my visibility increased, I became recognized as a thought leader. I wrote op-eds for various publications, including the *New York Times* and the online publishing platform *Medium*.

Staff from *The Guardian* and Equality Now stood by my side, attending meetings and covering my speeches. I believe *The*

Guardian's unusual involvement was primarily due to individuals on their team (such as Maggie O'Kane) who were deeply passionate about eradicating FGM. Despite the risks, they took on the campaign and helped significantly propel the visibility and progress of anti-FGM initiatives.

I wrote a few articles for *The Guardian* as a guest contributor. Getting paid a very small stipend for these articles did not make me feel good, but I needed any money I could earn. I worried others would use these payments as proof that I was a sellout and was doing this only for income. People did not know or believe I was selling most of the gold I had inherited from my mum to sustain myself and the work we were doing. When I launched the petition, I had never been paid for my activism or for appearances at the public events I had attended to support it. It had all come out of my own pocket. This is where my issue with money and the FGM campaign started. I have always been very sensitive about money, even though I know I deserve to be paid, because this has become my life work.

I decided to take the FGM campaign to the Gambia in 2014 through my organization Safe Hands for Girls, which I will talk about shortly. Prior to that, we had worked to engage youth on their issues and concerns online. Now we needed a grassroots in-person, education-oriented anti-FGM effort where we could talk openly and honestly with religious leaders, families, and the practitioners themselves. *The Guardian* accompanied us on our trips and documented our activities. This brought further visibility and support to our cause. Working in the Gambia felt like a breath of fresh air, as I was surrounded by human rights activists who now embraced my passion for eliminating FGM.

I loved what I did, and the inability to reveal it to my family had been a heavy burden. As time passed and my work grew increasingly successful, hiding it from my family became impossible. The media attention and recognition forced them to acknowledge my activism, though their understanding remained limited. Even now, they struggle to grasp fully the extent of my efforts and sometimes require me to provide answers to questions. However, my sister Fatoumata in Atlanta learned not to judge and to accept me for who I am.

Even today, my family occasionally stumbles upon one of my online videos and calls to remind me of who I am and request that I cover up more. My brothers refuse to tolerate negative comments about me, staunchly defending our bond. Each one of them echoes my father's famous proclamation about me: "We did not create her, but she is our blood, and we won't cast her aside." Nowadays, when the pressure becomes unbearable, I reach out to my siblings and my father and explain my perspective to ease their worries and foster understanding. It is not always easy, but I am grateful for their acceptance.

My relationship with my husband deteriorated entirely as I became a public figure. After many years, I finally mustered the courage to inform my family that I was going to get a divorce. Still, they dismissed my claim, thinking I was angry or upset. They finally comprehended my seriousness when I insisted they prepare themselves for an unmarried Jaha or, worse, a dead Jaha. No matter what, my family has always had an unwavering desire to protect me. Despite the world being against them and their own views, they decided that they should leave me alone, or risk losing me.

On the other hand, my husband saw my desire for a divorce as a betrayal. He still believes that if he had not allowed me to get an education or go to work, then I might have stayed in the marriage. I have heard comments from his family about how they warned him not to allow me to get an education. They firmly believe that who I am today is an outcome of the independence he gave me. What he and his family fail to understand is that getting an education and working kept me alive and gave me hope.

After the divorce, I knew I needed a change in location. While I had a home in the Gambia, I also needed a stable base in the United States for myself and my children. I moved away from Atlanta in

May 2017. My past was still intertwined with my ex-husband, and the home we had built together in Atlanta constantly reminded me of a chapter I wished to put behind me. The need for independence and the desire to escape judgment fueled my choice to distance myself and venture into a world where my decisions were solely my own, where I was unencumbered by the pressures of family and the community.

Life brought me temporarily back to New York City, the bustling city that had once overwhelmed me. But this time, it was different. My experiences had taught me to appreciate the essence of freedom. As it turned out, it was in New Jersey that I found my sanctuary. New Jersey offered me a chance to raise my kids in an excellent school system, something I valued immensely. It was a place where I could provide them with opportunities and a sense of security. As I settled into my new life, the charms of New Jersey unfolded before me. It had a different vibe, was not as messy as New York City, and the weather felt closer to that of Atlanta and the Gambia. The apartments were more spacious, allowing me the luxury of having breathing space, something I had longed for as someone who is claustrophobic. The area was green in summer and full of nature, something I had missed.

I continued my work in the Gambia and the United States. While fulfilling, it brought conflicts and challenges. My growing public persona and the attention I received created tensions with some of the people I worked with. Looking back, I realize I failed to acknowledge the contributions of others, to ensure they received the recognition they deserved. I inadvertently strained relationships and left well-intentioned individuals feeling invisible. As I continue to navigate this complex journey, I recognize the need to address the imbalance in attention and recognition within the movement. No one should feel overshadowed or diminished by the success of others. I have learned the value of humility, inclusivity, of uplifting the voices of all those who fight for justice. Though I may have made mistakes, I remain committed to doing better and making amends.

While my public role continues to evolve, I strive to uphold the values that initially propelled me into this fight. These values include honoring the dignity of all people, approaching difficult issues with love and empathy, and protecting women and children. These values serve as a constant reminder that I must always maintain sight of the impact I can have and the responsibility I bear. My journey has been filled with both triumphs and tribulations. Still, my unwavering dedication to end FGM and child marriages remains at the forefront of my heart and mind.

I always remember what we stand for. We offer up safe hands for girls.

Chapter 11

Safe Hands for Girls

IN ATLANTA OUR CLANDESTINE movement had taken shape. Women from diverse backgrounds, bound by a common cause, had united to combat the horrors of FGM and child marriage and to help women and children in need. We had formed a tight-knit underground network, offering support to those affected. As the years passed, our impact grew, and in 2013 we organized formally. A year later, we were recognized as a 501(c)(3) nonprofit organization, and Safe Hands for Girls was officially and legally born.

Our name holds a profound significance, and I can vividly recall the moment it came into being. As we searched for a name that encapsulated our purpose, one of our male supporters suggested Safe Hands for Girls. The instant he uttered those words, silence enveloped the room. It was as though the universe itself was speaking through him; the name resonated deeply within us all.

The name Safe Hands for Girls captures the essence of our mission: to be a sanctuary for girls who have endured FGM, offering them a refuge in times of despair. We want them to feel secure and protected, as if they are enveloped in safe hands, when they come to us seeking help and support.

The name holds another layer of significance because it speaks of transformation. The hands that once inflicted violence and pain on innocent girls find redemption, turning from agents of harm into safe hands, nurturing a new era of compassion and understanding. The name represents hope, resilience, and the possibility of healing and change. Safe Hands for Girls was destined to transform individual lives and entire communities, not only for the girls and women who had been subjected to FGM, but also for the men and women who had forced the practice on infants, girls, and women who had no choice.

As we embraced our new nonprofit status, we realized it reflected our ultimate goal: to empower girls and women to stand tall, unafraid, and strong. To walk confidently, knowing they were in safe hands within our organization and their communities. Safe Hands for Girls has become more than just a name. It has become our anthem, a rallying cry that unites us in purpose. With every step we take, we reaffirm our commitment to protect girls' well-being and rights, nurture their dreams and aspirations, and stand as guardians against the shadows of FGM, child marriage, and gender-based violence. While our name carries a weight of responsibility, it has become a beacon of hope, lighting our path. In every encounter, whether with doctors, religious leaders, lawmakers, or survivors, we embody the essence of our name.

In addition to our work in the United States, we also developed a strong online presence for youth in the Gambia to better understand their needs and issues. In 2014, we took our work in person to the Gambia, aligning ourselves with the United Nations Convention on the Rights of the Child to pursue our goals. As members of a survivor-led project, we empathized with the lived experiences of victims, knowing FGM robs them of health, happiness, and the opportunity to fulfill their dreams.

We took our online experience with young people and built an in-person youth movement to inspire and educate them. In schools nationwide, we established clubs to foster a new generation of change agents. We empowered young girls and boys to stand up for their communities, protect one another, and be the architects of a better future. We traveled to every corner of the Gambia, conducting training sessions and workshops. We knew reaching the hearts and minds of young people was pivotal in creating lasting change. Their enthusiasm and passion ignited a spark within us.

From the start, the strength of our organization has come from remarkable people. Lisa Camara has been with me from the beginning and serves as the country director in the Gambia. She is also a survivor of FGM. Her unparalleled dedication to the cause of eradicating FGM stands out prominently. Lisa is tireless, often doing more for the cause than anyone I know. Despite our challenges, where we encounter deception or misinformation, Lisa remains patient. While I tend to react with frustration, Lisa understands how to engage with the communities. She possesses an innate ability to listen to them, a trait I admire deeply. She is a nurturing mother figure, always the grounding force when the rest of us occasionally let loose. Lisa's unique strengths have been instrumental to our success in the Gambia. Without her, our progress would not have been possible.

Maria Saine, who reminds me of myself in many ways, started as a young volunteer and then helped build most of our programs in the Gambia. With Lisa, she helped grow our organization while I was away building our global presence. She is now a lawyer, and although no longer with Safe Hands, she is someone we always count on, especially for free legal advice. Muhamed Dibbasey joined Safe Hands around the same time as Maria and continues to play a strong part of our organization. He demonstrates that you do not have to be a woman to understand the suffering of women and girls.

One of the most powerful trips for me with Safe Hands took place while I was celebrating my twenty-sixth birthday, and it unspooled in a way I could have never imagined. We took the youth campaign to Gambissara, accompanied by a crew filming a documentary about my fight against FGM. As we traversed various regions of the country on our way to the town, a whirlwind of emotions consumed me. Memories of my last visit to Gambissara haunted me; it was for my mother's funeral. I did not have pleasant memories to fall back on and was apprehensive about discussing such a culturally sensitive topic with people I had known as a young girl.

As I have shared, Gambissara is a bastion of tradition in the Gambia. No youth organization had ever ventured there to address the issue of FGM, mainly due to the town residents' deeply entrenched beliefs. Such is the intensity of this conviction that FGM had a staggering prevalence rate of over 99 percent in the town at that time. Whenever I had voiced previously my intention to revisit Gambissara, the reactions had ranged from disbelief to concern. Nonetheless, the reception was heartwarming. I felt like royalty returning home. Traditional dancers and musicians welcomed us, their drums resonating in our hearts. Schoolchildren—a surprisingly higher number of girls than boys—thronged to meet us.

Engaging the women of Gambissara on the topic of FGM was no easy task. The men, fiercely protective of their women, had to be absent from the conversations. After they left for prayers, the atmosphere became conducive to open dialogue. The women unveiled their thoughts about FGM and our organization's mission. This was the first time there was an open debate about FGM in my hometown, which was amazing. Here is the transcript of a conversation we recorded:

WOMAN #1: *If a woman is not circumcised, how will the baby be delivered? Hmm? The child's head won't fit through. Circumcision is not a problem. If a woman is not circumcised, the child cannot be delivered. Circumcision is not a problem. I myself, sitting in this chair, I know. I have delivered twins, and I know how every child is delivered.*

WOMAN #2: *I think we circumcise our girls because we do not have the right medication to ease delivery. Women can deliver even if they are not circumcised.*

WOMAN #1: *Listen, if the girl child is not circumcised, then she cannot give birth. So, stop it.*

WOMAN #3: *We have heard from our ancestors that it is an Islamic obligation and a tradition worth practicing.*

WOMAN #4: *Did you ever question it?*

WOMAN #3: *No.*

WOMAN #4: *Why?*

WOMAN #2: *Because we are not educated. We are not versed in the Koran or English.*

ME: *You know, in more developed countries, they do not practice circumcision. Just as we view uncircumcised girls as a problem, they see circumcision of girls as a problem.*

WOMAN #1: *We have different beliefs. We believe that if a woman is not circumcised, birth will be difficult. Since I was born, that is how it was.*

WOMAN #2: *If proper health-care services and expertise would help women deliver without complications, if we get the right medical help, we will stop the practice.*

ME: *The lack of basic health care is a huge contributor to the issue of FGM. You know Gambissara doesn't even have a good hospital. This is our first time coming, but we plan to come back and work with you.*

WOMAN #2: *We can only stop if the elders of our village, including the chief and Imams, asked us to stop. Or else we will never stop.*[5]

It was clear that some women had entrenched themselves in their views, while others were more open. On this same trip, I spoke with one of the cutters in the village. She was the same woman who had performed FGM on me when I was a child; she and her sisters had carried out all the cuttings for my family. She had been good friends with my mum. My mum had loved this lady, and I had grown up loving her, too. She was like a second mother to all the children in my family.

Because of this mutual love, I thought making her understand how much pain FGM had caused me might lead her to rethink the practice and stop cutting. Here is how our conversation went:

SHE: *How are you? Look at you.*

ME: *The FGM you perform on these girls seals their vaginas. It is known that when you seal a woman, it is painful on her wedding night. So, how do you feel about it?*

SHE: *When you have no clitoris, that is when you are clean and pure in Islam, and sex is more enjoyable for the man.*

She proceeded to show me how the cutting was done.

SHE: *When she holds the child like this . . . Then I will hold the thing that is supposed to be cut. Twist it and then cut. I say, "Bismillah Rahmani Rahim" and then apply the powdered medication. After two hours, you can bathe her, and when the child urinates twice, it is done.*

ME: *You mentioned that if a woman is not circumcised, she is considered not clean. Why do you say the person is not clean?*

SHE: *When a woman is not circumcised, it itches. If the thing underneath is not removed, the hand will always be down there scratching.*

ME: *Many Gambians now know that FGM is not about cleanliness. Neither does it help when making love, but rather, it hurts. The first time I was supposed to have sex with my husband, they had to cut me open, and I was told to have sex that day. It was very painful.*

SHE: *Did that happen in America?*[6]

By that time, I knew our conversation would not change her thinking or actions. But I still loved her. When I left, we hugged and she said, "I think of you all the time." As much as I wanted to be angry and blame her, she was also a victim. The tradition had been passed on to her, and she had passed it on to her daughter, and now her daughter was passing it on to her eighteen-year-old daughter.

Our organization's work started going global. With limited funding, we had to make our voice as loud as possible. That meant going beyond the United States and the Gambia. While we could not directly implement programs in other countries, we could use the power of our online communities and collaboration with on-the-ground organizations in other nations to promote change.

In those countries where FGM and child marriage were prevalent, we aimed to shift practices and norms from within communities through billboard campaigns, radio broadcasts, and direct engagement with religious leaders. We knew that lasting change required the involvement of religious leaders. We partnered with Al-Azhar University in Egypt, an institution of higher learning renowned for its expertise in Islamic jurisprudence and at the forefront of the scholarly debate over the past two decades about FGM's legitimacy. The overwhelming consensus among Al-Azhar scholars is that FGM is a traditional custom, not a religious requirement, and should be banned. In our partnership, we simplified the university's message that Islam did not require FGM so that it would reach more people.

We organized important summits to propel our cause forward. The Dakar Summit held in June 2019 in Senegal was the first African summit on FGM and child marriage, and it reinforced the bridge between Africa and the world in order to accelerate the implementation of a zero-tolerance policy on these practices. It was a historic moment for our campaign. We brought together religious leaders, activists, survivors, lawmakers, and government agencies throughout Africa to ensure that FGM and child marriage become relics of the past by 2030. We also held a United States Summit to facilitate a cross-sectoral approach to ending FGM in the United States and internationally.

One focus of our global efforts was with health care professionals.

We contacted doctors, educating them about cultural sensitivity and the importance of approaching FGM cases with empathy and understanding. In the United States and Gambia, we sought to create a ripple effect by meeting in person with doctors to empower them with knowledge about how to handle FGM cases with sensitivity. For example, in the United States we had heard stories of Somalian women who felt humiliated and traumatized by doctors' insensitivity. Doctors in communities with significant immigrant populations needed to understand the implications of FGM and how to address it effectively.

We have also been involved in spotlighting fundamental women's rights issues and the contributions of women internationally through our collaborative efforts. International Women's Day holds a special place in our hearts as we celebrate the contributions of women across the globe and shed light on the often unnoticed work they do. We also observe the Day of the African Child, which is dedicated to showcasing children's talents through art and providing them with a platform to voice their concerns and issues. We commemorate annually the International Day of Zero Tolerance for Female Genital Mutilation, reiterating our commitment to ending FGM and gender-based violence. The FGM Media Award is a special day when we recognize and reward tireless activists working diligently to eradicate FGM, gender-based violence, and child marriage in the Gambia.

While we promoted change internationally, we also stepped up our efforts in the Gambia. I found myself as the organization's public face and advocated for change at the highest levels of government, which resulted in the 2015 ban on FGM in the Gambia and its subsequent illegality under the Women's Act 2010. I will share the details of this effort in later pages of this book. However, the law still needed to be widely understood and followed across the country.

Our efforts have included community and school outreach to educate the Gambian population about the law and the penalties for violating it. The school outreach program entails visiting schools across the Gambia. In the schools, we conduct training sessions for young advocates, empowering them with knowledge about FGM, child marriage, teenage pregnancy, gender-based violence, and the Women's Act. These young advocates are vital to changing perceptions within their communities. Additionally, we provide intensive training to young students on other issues impacting their daily lives, enabling them to become informed and proactive agents of change.

As our focus on advocacy evolved, we realized addressing FGM alone was insufficient. Women's economic empowerment in the Gambia was vital in dismantling the oppressive chains that held women back. Many women confided in us that their inability to leave abusive situations or to protect their daughters from FGM was due to financial constraints. This realization led to the birth of the Community Garden Initiative. We began supporting women who had once subjected girls to FGM but had chosen to break free from that cycle. By empowering them through gardening, we offered them not just nourishment from the vegetables they grew but also the nourishment of financial independence. They could now send their daughters to school, an opportunity once denied them, and this served to break the chains of poverty and oppression.

Then came the dark days of the pandemic. COVID-19 brought a new wave of challenges, particularly for women and girls. With lockdowns in place, girls faced an increased risk of violence, and women were confined to their homes, unable to escape abusive circumstances. In response, we initiated global self-defense programs, empowering women to protect themselves and stand firm in the face of adversity.

Our journey with Safe Hands for Girls has not been without its struggles. Financial hardships tested the dedication of our staff. Still, our shared passion and commitment kept us together as a close-knit family. Despite challenges, we remained focused on the grassroots level, ensuring our message reached the communities we aimed to serve. Even as this book was being written, forces in the Gambia and other countries were trying to overturn laws that protect girls and women from FGM. Our advocacy efforts at Safe Hands are never-ending.

Personally, I have grown as a leader by becoming more self-aware. My team often refers to me as "crazy" for my seemingly reckless determination and insistence on pursuing what I believe in. This particular attitude has caused myriad issues within the group, as staff members perceive me as unreasonable at times. My relentless nature, which could keep me awake for days focusing on our mission, has been a source of both admiration and frustration among the team. I am doing better, or at least I'm trying. Finding the balance between passion and pragmaticism can be challenging.

Whatever our programs, it all comes down to helping individuals. The essence of Safe Hands for Girls lies not in the glamour of social media or global events but in the grassroots, where we connect with people at their most vulnerable moments. We have cried with survivors, laughed with young advocates, and celebrated each triumph as a family united in purpose.

Our work with women and girls crosses all ages. In the Gambia, we started a community garden for a group of older women, who quickly became my family. They were women who had children and grandchildren, but they call me their mother, and their problems were my problems. When their community faced challenges, they approached me for assistance, and I did everything I could to support them. These remarkable women, who could be my grandmothers, have impacted me deeply. The daughters of these women are now protected from the harmful practice of female genital mutilation because of our work. And their children have the opportunity to attend school and pursue a brighter future.

Maryam, a brilliant, beautiful young woman currently studying in the United States, joined Safe Hands when she was fourteen. Like me, she is outspoken. Though she never underwent FGM, she became passionate about the cause, recognizing the potential dangers she might have faced as a Gambian girl. She is remarkably articulate, channeling her passion into advocacy efforts on television and radio. Maryam's fervor mirrors my own, but mine stemmed from personal experience and hers emerged from empathy.

Another touching story is that of a young girl in the Gambia whose father chose to spare her from FGM because of our outreach efforts. Whenever we visit her community, she proudly sports a T-shirt from one of our previous programs. We call her our "T-shirt baby." Whenever we have activities, we send her T-shirts for her collection. Some girls collect rock band T-shirts; she collects T-shirts from our movement. Despite being only ten years old, she dreams of following in my footsteps. It moves me greatly to watch this young activist in the making. It gives me such hope for the future.

These connections, forged through our shared struggle, have enriched my life in ways I cannot adequately express. Whenever I consider giving up, I think of these individuals who have become part of my extended family, and I find renewed strength to continue our mission. However, it is essential to acknowledge that this work is not easy. My emotional investment in every person I encounter makes their challenges my own. I feel the world's weight on my shoulders as people turn to me for help in times of crisis. The burden can become overwhelming, and the responsibility seems too great for one person to bear alone.

I have also met individuals from diverse backgrounds and sexual orientations who have become integral to my life. Each encounter has deepened my understanding of the human experience and reaffirmed my commitment to fighting for justice. The connections I have formed remind me that this work is not just about me—it is about building a network of support, passing on knowledge, and ensuring the sustainability of our efforts. This work is about so much more than individual achievements. The collective impact of our actions, magnified by the ripple effect of change, shapes the destinies of daughters worldwide.

As I look back on our journey, I am humbled and grateful for the privilege of serving as the vessel for the Safe Hands for Girls' mission. Our work is far from over, and the path ahead remains challenging. Still, I am confident our collective dedication and unwavering bonds will continue to pave the way for a world free from the darkness of FGM and gender-based violence.

Our legacy will not be measured in headlines or accolades but in the lives of the countless girls and women who will stand tall, unafraid, and empowered, knowing they are in safe hands. Safe hands, however, need to be attached to a body of legislation to be effective. Our unexpected victories in the Gambia made it possible.

Chapter 12

Unexpected Victories

I RETURNED TO THE GAMBIA in 2014 to organize a youth summit in collaboration with multiple organizations, including Think Young Women and my own nonprofit, Safe Hands for Girls. I was twenty-five at the time. For the first time, we brought together young people from all across the country to discuss FGM. At the time none of us expected legislative changes related to FGM in the Gambia, because there was no indication this was possible soon. Our primary goal was to foster advocacy and raise awareness.

We focused on youth because we believed that the older generations had largely formed their opinions on this matter and that it would be more productive to engage with younger individuals, the future mothers and fathers. Previous efforts to end FGM in the Gambia had not considered young people as potential influencers in stopping the practice. Older individuals, such as grandmothers or elder aunts, usually influenced the decision to have FGM performed on girls, and so young people had not been targeted in awareness campaigns. Our primary aim now was prevention, since we could not change what had already transpired. This time around we hoped to safeguard the next generations from this practice. Our strategy was simple: a youth-led initiative for youth.

The summit kicked off at the Paradise Suites Hotel in Serrekunda with an opening ceremony that included government officials and representatives from many organizations that had been working against FGM in the Gambia for years. The three-day event featured interactive sessions where FGM was discussed from health, human rights, and religious perspectives.

The summit was funded by Human Dignity Foundation, under its executive director, Mary Healy. Mary was one of the first donors to Safe Hands, and she understood our mission and treated us with so much dignity and respect. She was more than a donor; she was an ally who cared about the issues, cared about us, and even opened her home to us. For example, when Maria, who was on our staff, wanted to pursue further studies, Mary helped her enroll in Trinity University in Ireland and also helped support her while she lived there. Over the years, I became very close to Mary and her family; her children are like little sisters to me. The chair of Human Dignity Foundation is Dr. John Climax. I became good friends with his son, Joshua, who has often visited me in the Gambia.

Before the summit began, we engaged journalists, despite a ban on discussing FGM in the media. The event garnered considerable local and international media attention, notably from *The Guardian*, which was there to document it as part of its documentary project *Jaha's Promise*. One local journalist asked me about my aspirations for the Gambia. I responded that I wished to see a ban on FGM. This statement, subsequently featured on the front pages of newspapers in the Gambia, was met with skepticism and online insults, as many believed such a change was impossible.

Outside of the Gambia, I had garnered a generally positive reputation. I had stepped into the public eye, achieved considerable results in the United States, founded Safe Hands in Atlanta, and begun its operations in the Gambia. I was seen as a formidable force. However, within the Gambia, I was met with suspicion and accused of being a puppet of the West.

This perception was not just that of people who were pro-FGM. It hurt to be misunderstood by some of our own partners in the fight and accused of exploiting the issue for personal gain. Some speculated that my involvement would wane once the "funding ran dry." Contrary to assumptions, I was not funded by any external entities. My genuine passion for the cause and desire to give back to my country were my driving forces.

It was very important to me to be an on-the-ground activist within the Gambia. I felt that because people perceived my efforts as serving Western interests, if I could not initiate change from within my home country, then my efforts would not seem authentic. It did not feel right to advocate from the comfort of America, where I was essentially preaching to the choir. There, my work with various government entities was met with agreement and support. However, the Gambia was where the actual work was needed. Considering my personal history with FGM in the Gambia, it felt natural to return and contribute to change.

After the youth summit, we collaborated with Think Young Women to conduct various educational activities throughout the country. We set up booths in areas with high foot traffic, like streets and markets, to disseminate information on FGM and engage the public in conversations about it. Initially, our approach was met with resistance. FGM was a deeply rooted issue and was often brushed under the carpet. Discussing it publicly was considered taboo. We were often seen as disrespectful and labeled negatively, but we persevered.

Both young Gambian men and women were involved in these grassroots efforts. They came to us through various channels. Many volunteers attended the events we organized, while others met us during our campaigns in the streets. As time passed, some joined through social media outreach or personal mentoring requests. To my surprise, men made up almost half of our supporters. Most of them joined because they genuinely believed the practice should stop. Some were passionate about human rights, while others wanted to ally with women.

One such man was Modou Lamin Davies, a law student, who became a program manager for Safe Hands. He later co-founded Beyond Advocacy, which uses an empowerment-based self-defense model to help women and girls protect themselves from violence.

Another male advocate was Sait Matty Jaw, a human rights defender, who helped register Safe Hands in the Gambia and remains a prominent supporter of gender rights in the country.

Two of our staff, Lisa and Maria, were instrumental in conducting grassroots work in various communities. They bravely ventured into the heart of these areas to engage in discussions with the locals. Sometimes their efforts were met with hostility and fear, and this even led to them being chased out of villages. It was an emotionally taxing endeavor, with instances when it was impossible for them not to take things personally, as they felt the weight of their experiences.

While our organization and volunteers engaged in grassroots activities, I employed another strategy. My goal was to meet personally with President Jammeh to ask him to ban FGM. On this quest for a meeting, I was accompanied by *Guardian* videographer Louis Leeson and my cousin Fatoumata, who was living in the Gambia. I chose not to include any of my Safe Hands team in order to protect them from potential dangers. I was willing to take certain risks myself, but I could not bear the thought of putting them in jeopardy from the government. The Gambia was a dangerous and hostile place at that time if you angered the president and his supporters.

Although President Jammeh eluded our first attempt at a meeting, I was granted an audience with his ministers. During this critical meeting, the minister of justice, Mama Fatima Singhateh, expressed strong reservations about banning FGM, fearing the effect this would have on the older generation of women in the country. The consensus among the ministers oscillated between a firm belief in preserving the tradition and a cautious openness to dialogue. There was also an underlying hesitancy to embrace my advocacy, primarily due to the uncertainty surrounding President Jammeh's stance on the issue. Given his known propensity to champion cultural traditions and reject Western influences, his ministers seemed skeptical about him endorsing an FGM ban. I left the venue almost in tears, feeling demoralized.

Despite that meeting, we forged onward, fueled by an unwavering belief in the necessity for change. I became deeply immersed in the political and social milieu of the Gambia and forged alliances with several government insiders, including Omar Saine, the minister of health, and Lamin Manga, the minister of presidential affairs. Saine became not only a reliable source of information on the pressing issues concerning women's health conditions in the country but also a cherished friend. Alongside him, I developed a rapport with Yankouba Colley, mayor of Serekunda, the largest city in the Gambia, who generously supported our cause. My connections to these government officials, who were quite close to the president, proved invaluable.

At a certain juncture, my activities caught the attention of the Ministry of Interior. This resulted in unnerving encounters with agencies notorious for their brutal methods. I was summoned to the National Intelligence Agency (NIA) and the Ministry of Interior for interrogation. I had heard numerous stories about Yankuba Badjie, the head of the NIA, and the agency's alleged involvement in the deaths of many individuals. Consequently, I believed this could be my end.

Whenever I heard Badjie's name, an image would form in my mind of a villain, like the ones we often see in movies. I am unsure why I imagined him in such a way, but I had a preconceived idea about his appearance. When my cousin and I arrived at the NIA to meet the director, we were escorted to his office, an imposing space with large screens belonging to a vast surveillance system. I suspected they intended to intimidate me with this display. They were successful.

When Badjie entered the room, he was not the towering figure I had expected. In fact, he was shorter than me. In a candid moment, I expressed my surprise at his appearance and even complimented him on his looks. We shared laughter, and what was supposed to be an interrogation turned into an engaging conversation about my recent return to the country and my objectives. Quite unexpectedly, by the end of our meeting, our interaction had evolved into a "friendship" characterized by camaraderie and even lighthearted jests about his appearance and reputation.

Our bond grew over time. He would alert me if I or any of my team faced potential dangers. I recall one incident when social activist Sait Matty Jaw was first released from jail in the Gambia. Director Badjie informed me of Sait's impending rearrest and urged me to ensure his safety. On another occasion, he shielded me during a session at the Gambian embassy in New York. At that time, I was quite vocal about criticizing the Gambian government. He called me to caution restraint, since despite being continents away, the Gambia had an extensive network of "supporters" and influence in New York.

One instance when Badjie came to the rescue really stands out in my mind. We were detained by a top NIA agent, a man notorious for his close relationship with President Jammeh and his involvement in numerous dark chapters of the regime. We were suspected of intending to expose the grim realities of life in the Gambia during the regime, a period characterized by rampant human rights violations, the suppression of freedom of the press, and even a leader boasting about curing AIDS. Under President Jammeh's rule, people often disappeared without a trace, and their grim fates were later revealed. Given my advocacy, I feared I might meet a similar end.

Fortunately, Badjie intervened upon hearing of my detention. He vouched for my intentions and my background, effectively defusing the situation. When we spoke, he jokingly inquired about my audacious attempt to meet the president. After our conversation, he instructed his agents to release us and provide us with shelter, food, and fuel. Furthermore, he facilitated the establishment of a communication channel between me and the president, enabling a dialogue that might not have been possible otherwise.

A little while after this incident with the NIA agent, I was engaged in media training in the Gambia when I received distressing news about my children being in an accident in Atlanta. Without hesitation, I flew back to the United States. As soon as I got there, I received the call that I finally had a meeting with President Jammeh. After confirming that my children were fine, I hopped back on a plane. This whirlwind of events within forty-eight hours led to a significant meeting, as I found an unexpected ally in the president.

In the past, President Jammeh had showcased an agenda focused on aiding women and girls. He initiated free education for girls and advocated for gender equality in primary and secondary schools. His support for girls and women seemed substantial, especially compared to previous leaders of the Gambia. Nonetheless, his reign was marred by numerous human rights violations, including the sexual exploitation of young girls and women. Despite some progressive policies, his actions betrayed a darker, exploitative nature, which overshadowed the positive aspects of his legacy.

I disapproved of his actions, but as president, he was unavoidable. The power was in his hands. My priority was delivering my message and ensuring the banning of FGM in the Gambia. I knew I needed to tread carefully, and I realized being an activist sometimes meant navigating complex and corrupt environments and engaging with people whose fundamental morality was questionable.

President Jammeh treated me respectfully, likening me to a daughter. Our conversation ranged from the Gambia's future to his controversial claims about curing AIDS. I understood the gravity of disagreeing with someone like President Jammeh and maintained a careful demeanor throughout our interaction. My ability to navigate such challenging scenarios is one of my notable attributes. I always strive to connect with the human aspect of the individuals I encounter, even in life-threatening situations.

This is one facet of who I am that always baffles people. Many say my values should not have allowed me to work with someone like President Jammeh. But in our world, where so many things are wrong and so many people are bad, hope for two hundred million girls was greater than any misgivings I had about working with President Jammeh. I knew legislation would not happen without him. Over the years, both in my personal life and professional work, I have learned to extract myself and my emotions for the greater good of the work we do. This is not always easy for me, and there are days when I hate myself for not standing up to all those people, but I have learned to choose the battles and not dilute the work.

During our meeting, President Jammeh expressed a commitment to addressing women's issues and fighting against FGM. He never indicated that he would institute a ban. So, much to my surprise, on November 23, 2015, he announced a ban on FGM. It was an unexpected and amazing victory. I cannot begin to tell you the feelings that encompassed me. It had been a long and hard fight for so many of us.

Shortly after that, a 2015 amendment to the Women's Act 2010 criminalizing the practice of FGM and stipulating severe punishment for violators became law. My father was the first person to call me with the news that the Gambian government had passed the law. Back when I took a leave of absence from my bank job to help lead the fight against FGM, he had told me I was wasting my life. He'd admonished me about never having time for my husband and children, and he'd been adamant that FGM would never end. In his view, my fight was hopeless. I will never forget my dad's response to the new law: "Okay, maybe you're not wasting your life, after all."

My relationship with the Gambian government had been a double-edged sword. While it had facilitated my safety and granted me access to powerful changemakers, it had also brewed suspicion among other activists. There were rumors about me having intimate relationships with high-ranking officials, which were unequivocally untrue. I was married at the time, and even when single, I had never engaged in that type of behavior. Despite the negative perceptions, I believed some ministers genuinely desired to see the laws change and to have FGM banned.

Additionally, my ability to foster connections and initiate dialogues with higher-ups in the government was misconstrued as my exploiting my appearance or using my femininity as a tool to get ahead. It is true that my looks, coincidentally, resemble those of the type of woman President Jammeh was known to prefer. This might have played a role in furthering our cause, but it was never a calculated strategy.

Despite criticisms and attempts to discredit our contributions and me personally, I know our relentless collaborative efforts were a catalytic force behind this monumental change. We were interested not in seeking recognition but in witnessing the tangible results of our hard work: women and girls protected from the harmful practice of FGM. As time passed, we observed that the law against FGM remained steadfast even under new governance, signifying a victory for every girl in our country. It was a testament to our team's perseverance and the undeniable impact we had made in our nation's history.

Despite the passage of a law banning FGM, we knew legislative action alone would not stop the practice. It was crucial to commence an educational campaign to complement the new law, given its top-down implementation due to the dictatorial regime. Personally, I felt leading an educational initiative in the Gambia at this time would place me in jeopardy.

I left the country a few days after President Jammeh announced the ban and avoided returning until his departure from office. Given his reputation, I worried he would want "payback," and I feared that rejecting any form of relationship he might propose would put my life in danger. I did my part outside the country, participating in interviews to spread awareness and insights. My team and other organizations led grassroots efforts.

So, less than a year after the youth summit, legislation banning FGM was enacted in the Gambia. This turn of events proved wrong the many skeptics and critics who saw me as a naive Western agent. The undeniable fact remains that our efforts contributed significantly to the Gambia's decision to outlaw FGM under the leadership of President Jammeh, despite his infamy as a dictator. Those who campaigned against FGM before us were courageous and their efforts were vital, enabling our youthful vigor and innovative strategies to reinvigorate the movement. Despite media restrictions under President Jammeh's regime, we boldly collaborated with journalists, training them to tell human interest stories about FGM. Our relentless campaign succeeded because we networked strategically, even within President Jammeh's cabinet.

With the banning of FGM, the crucial issue that needed to be addressed was the banning of child marriage in the Gambia. First Lady Zainab Jammeh wielded considerable influence over her husband and facilitated the passage of the child marriage ban. Her involvement and the dedication she showed to this cause were undeniable. My organization actively participated in advocacy campaigns and assisted in drafting the necessary bill, collaborating with the National Assembly of the Gambia and the First Lady's office. In July 2016 the Children's Amendment Act was enacted. It prohibited child marriage and established eighteen as the minimum age for marriage.

I kept a personal distance from these discussions. Due to my past experiences with child marriage and my ongoing marriage with the father of my children, it was a topic I found too difficult to talk about. It was too raw. But as I took the campaign against FGM global, I realized I needed also to talk about being a child bride. Telling my full story with stark honesty and successfully working toward change now catapulted me to the uncomfortable place of being seen as more than a survivor and an activist. I was now being called a hero.

Chapter 13

Becoming a "Hero"

I HAVE NEVER SOUGHT TO BE hailed as a hero simply for doing what I believe is right. We possess a moral compass for a purpose: to differentiate right from wrong. The causes I champion hinge on this fundamental distinction. Despite the challenges, my efforts have been acknowledged and celebrated worldwide. This is a testament to the fact that unwavering belief in a cause, even in the face of adversity, eventually bears fruit, as it has for me.

My stance against FGM and child marriage initially made me a pariah within my community and family. Now I stand as one of my country's most esteemed figures. I have traversed the globe through my work, setting foot on every continent except Australia. The journey to where I am now has been astonishing. Following the FGM ban, I gained both national and international recognition. Today any discourse on FGM inevitably mentions my contributions. My efforts continue to resonate globally. My alma mater even dedicated a classroom in my honor.

The media wields immense power. *The Guardian* was instrumental in amplifying my voice, letting me share my truth with a global audience. When this newspaper first highlighted my endeavors and campaigns, I faced constant online vitriol and became a hot topic of gossip. Initially, I braced myself for a perpetual uphill battle, wondering if people would ever grasp the essence of my mission.

Even though *The Guardian*'s actions stemmed from benevolent intentions, there were inadvertent detrimental effects from my collaboration with them. At times, the paper failed to comprehend the strain the vivid portrayal of my story in their articles exerted on my mental health. The relentless scrutiny and criticism from my family, coupled with the exacerbated anxiety due to the public nature of my narrative, became too much to bear. Despite this, there seemed to be an expectation of gratitude toward *The Guardian* for its publicity, leaving me grappling with discomfort and dissatisfaction regarding my position. But without *The Guardian*, our efforts would probably not have succeeded. I am forever indebted to it.

As time passed, the world began to appreciate the significance of my voice as a survivor and activist. In 2015 I was named a L'Oréal Paris Women of Worth honoree. This recognition marked one of the first acknowledgments of my work. It opened doors and introduced me to individuals passionate about supporting my cause. Over time, my bond with L'Oréal strengthened, and I became one of their international global brand ambassadors.

My work garnered further recognition when my Change.org petition gained traction. For instance, this led to numerous invitations to US government events. During President Obama's tenure, I visited the White House twice. I addressed the audience at the White House United State of Women Summit in 2016, where I shared the stage with the then vice president Joe Biden. Both President Barack Obama and First Lady Michelle Obama delivered speeches at this event, which also saw appearances by renowned personalities like Oprah Winfrey.

In 2016 I was also named one of *Time* magazine's 100 most influential people in the world. At that moment, I was unfamiliar with the significance of the Time100, and this prompted me to research it. To my astonishment, I found myself alongside such esteemed individuals as Barack Obama and Oprah Winfrey. Overwhelmed with joy, I exclaimed aloud, "Mama, I made it!" I felt on top of the world.

The Time100 Gala was a whirlwind of experiences. I mingled with incredible individuals who had also been recognized that year, watched Nicki Minaj perform live, and captured memories with several influential attendees. Interestingly, Donald Trump was present, given that this was the year he launched his presidential campaign. Although I identify as a Democrat and did not seek out a photograph with him, had Barack Obama been there, I would have pursued every opportunity for a picture with him. I shared my table with Trevor Noah and noted the number of guests eager for a photograph with him. The gala, hosted at Jazz at Lincoln Center, was covered extensively by the media in my homeland, and the news was met with immense pride there.

A very different experience was being appointed UN Women Goodwill Ambassador for Africa in 2018. Unlike the regular UN ambassadors, who do not represent a particular nation or region of the globe and are generally high-profile celebrities, I have had the opportunity to offer a unique perspective due to my experiences. My role has seen me traveling extensively and collaborating with dedicated individuals striving for global change. What I have cherished most in this role is my interactions with local communities worldwide, which consistently rejuvenates my spirit and my determination.

My appointment during Phumzile Mlambo-Ngcuka's tenure as executive director of UN Women and Alison Rowe's tenure as communications director signified that impactful ambassadors do not always have to be celebrities; sometimes those with genuine lived experiences make the most meaningful connections. Alison Rowe and I often traveled together, and we became good friends. I have learned a lot from her, and she continues to be a great source of support to me in what can often be a challenging environment. I owe a great deal to Phumzile Mlambo-Ngcuka, a mentor who has invested time and energy in me. Because I saw African women like her in leadership positions at the UN, I believed this was possible for me. I continue to count on both Phumzile and Alison for support whenever I feel lost.

Remarkably, a day after my United Nations appointment, I discovered that I had been nominated for the Nobel Peace Prize. I was

Attending my first day of school at the age of six, accompanied by my sister Fatoumata, who is three years older.
(Photo Credit: Jaha Dukureh Family Photo Album)

Here I am at the age of ten with my older sister Fatoumata.
(Photo Credit: Jaha Dukureh Family Photo Album)

Out in the field with my two sons,
Abu, age six, and Muhammed,
age eleven.
(Photo Credit: Alhagie Manka)

Enjoying a beautiful day in
the park in North Bergen, NJ,
close to my apartment with
my youngest son Abu and
daughter Khadija.
(Photo Credit: Selfie)

Visiting with a midwife named Ma Sarjo during Gambisara Outreach Campaign.
(Photo Credit: Louis Leeson)

Me pictured with Shelby Quast (middle) of Equality Now and Haddijattou Ceesay (left),
who was the program officer for Safe Hands for Girls.
(Photo Credit: Louis Leeson)

Encouraging young attendees at a youth conference in October of 2014.
(Photo Credit: Alhagie Manka)

Walking with supporters during one of my campaigns against FGM in Birikma,
one of the largest cities in The Gambia, in 2015.
(Photo Credit: Alhagie Manka)

Attendees of the National Islamic Conference on FGM in 2016.
(Photo Credit: Alhagie Manka)

Attending a conference organized for Muslim circumcisers in Liberia.
(Photo Credit: Alhagie Manka)

Greeting the Deputy Secretary of the United Nations while Alison Rowe,
who spearheads the Goodwill Ambassador Program at the UN, and Phumzile Mlambo-Ngcuka,
the former Executive Director of the UN (right), look on.
(Photo Credit: Jaha Dukureh)

Pictured with United States Senator Elizabeth Warren,
Americas Director of Equality Now, Shelby Quast, and Arichi Piyati.
(Photo Credit: Haddy Mbow)

With the late US Senator Harry Reid
in his office.
(Photo Credit: Haddy Mbow)

With the late US Representative
and civil rights leader John Lewis
at his DC office during my
change.org petition in 2014.
(Photo Credit: Haddy Mbow)

With former US Representative Joe Crowley, Shelby Quast of Equality Now, and Congresswoman Sheila Jackson Lee.
(Photo Credit: Haddy Mbow)

Sitting pretty in a photo session held during the Commission on the Status of Women at the United Nations.
(Photo Credit: Courtesy of Jaha Dukureh)

Serving as Co-Chair of the Interparty Committee during the presidential election in 2021
(Photo Credit: Alhagie Manka)

in Senegal, knee-deep in preparations for an FGM summit, when I stumbled upon the news online. The emotions I felt were overwhelming. The thought of a girl from a humble village in the Gambia, the smallest mainland African nation, becoming the youngest African Nobel Prize nominee was surreal. Learning that the person behind the nomination was a lawmaker from Norway added a personal touch to the already monumental honor, because I had met him during a screening of the documentary about me. The entire team and I were engulfed in many emotions that day. This nomination elevated my standing in the Gambia, garnered respect for my work, and increased global visibility for the movement to eradicate FGM and child marriage. When I was introduced as a Nobel Peace Prize nominee, I instantly noticed the shift in perceptions. It continues to this day.

That same year I was also deeply honored to receive the Eleanor Roosevelt Medal, which honors "individuals who embraced Eleanor Roosevelt's call to build a better world through humanitarian efforts in education, advocacy, social justice, and civil and human rights."[7] To be part of the group of amazing men and women who have received this award over the past thirty years was humbling.

But these honors always felt bittersweet. Whenever I received another accolade, my thoughts would wander to my mother, the beacon who had always believed in my potential. I was destined for greatness in her eyes, and she foresaw a different path for me than the one she had experienced in her own life. Her absence during these moments of recognition left a void no award could fill. I yearned to share them with the one person who truly understood my journey. It is a painful irony that the moments meant to celebrate my accomplishments were also filled with profound longing and grief.

I never set out on this journey to become a hero. The awards and accolades, while appreciated, were never the end goal. The essence of my journey is not about the public's perception but about staying true to myself, honoring my mother's memory, and striving to make a genuine impact. In a world that can sometimes place too much emphasis on fame and recognition, I aim to remain grounded and authentic, ensuring the humaneness in me is never overshadowed by the titles I bear.

As amazing as the global recognition has been, the honors that have come out of Africa and from the African diaspora have been particularly moving to me. I was named one of the 100 most influential Africans of 2017 by *New African* magazine; honored as the "Human Rights Activist, Humanitarian of the Year" at the seventh annual African Diaspora Awards; and identified as one of the Top 10 Africa Changemakers by YouthHubAfrica.

The most heartfelt and genuine affirmation of my positive impact came from my home village when, on my first trip back, I was welcomed back by a chorus of children singing the national anthem in my honor. This simple, genuine act was a more poignant validation than any glossy magazine feature or international accolade. My roots recognized my worth before the world did, and that is a memory I cherish deeply. Subsequent visits to the Gambia, especially the one I made during the presidential election in 2021, reaffirmed my status as a national hero. Places outside of the Gambia, such as Liberia, have greeted me with the same kindness, whether it was at a reception at the airport or during unexpected encounters on the streets with fans who recognized and admired me.

A recurring critique of me is that I am unaware of the influence I wield. It is not a matter of ignorance on my part but a conscious choice to remain grounded. I resist the urge to be idolized because I am acutely aware of my imperfections. Yes, I falter, and sometimes my decisions miss the mark, but I rise every day. As much as it is a pleasure to inspire others and be looked up to, there is a pressing weight to meet the expectations of an ever-watching public. Every action, every choice, every association is under scrutiny. Such unwarranted attention can be both dehumanizing and isolating. The larger the pedestal, the harder it is to retain one's sense of self.

That is particularly true when I am in the Gambia. During a

recent visit, I was overwhelmed by people telling me what I should do and how I should do it to maintain my reputation as a "hero" and further my political agenda. However, I know now that living authentically is vital to my physical, mental, and spiritual well-being. I will never return to the duality of who I was for so many years. I will not keep the real me hidden.

The most challenging aspect of being labeled a "hero" is that people assume they now know me, thanks to all the honors and media attention. Yes, they know about my efforts. They know I have shared a deeply personal story to bring awareness to two issues that devastate the lives of girls and women globally. Too often they fail to recognize I am human. Hero status tends to remove humanity. People blow up your mistakes into deep flaws, and your accomplishments become miracles.

Perhaps, the clearest example of what it has been like for me to be idolized as a hero is what happened when my story became the subject of the documentary film *Jaha's Promise*. I was only twenty-eight when it was released in 2017. While the film did a wonderful job chronicling my efforts to lead a successful campaign against the brutal practices that had once nearly destroyed my life, it did not go into the bad decisions I had made or my personality flaws. It was solely focused on me fulfilling my promise to get FGM banned.

Its release was met with critical acclaim, which helped to spread the message and inspired others to join the fight for gender equality and justice. The documentary also sparked criticism from some detractors, who accused me of monopolizing the FGM narrative. Naively, I did not realize it would also compel so many people to describe me as a hero. One reason I wrote this memoir was so that people would see me as a human, not a hero.

Chapter 14

The Making of *Jaha's Promise*

EVERY DAY I GET COMMENTS from people who have seen *Jaha's Promise*. Many tell me they were moved to tears. Others say they never really understood the issue before seeing the movie. Some call me a saint; others call me the devil. What astounds me is the reach and impact of this film throughout the world.

The visionaries behind the movie were Patrick Farrelly and Kate O'Callaghan, who produced, directed, and wrote it. When I met Patrick, he was on a project for *The Guardian* that entailed creating a series of short films on my efforts to lobby the Obama administration to acknowledge and address FGM in the United States. I think his description of why he wanted to make *Jaha's Promise* is better than any explanation I can give.

On the seventieth anniversary of the adoption of the Universal Declaration of Human Rights, Ciné-ONU, a European-wide initiative sponsored by the United Nations that entails regular film screenings and discussions relevant to UN issues, interviewed Patrick, and he said the following:

"As we were wrapping up our project, I found myself in awe of her indomitable spirit and felt an intrinsic need to explore her story further. When I asked her about her future plans, she mentioned her intention to head back to Africa to not only converse with her father, with whom she had never discussed the topic of FGM, but also to lead a formidable campaign aiming to eradicate FGM and child marriage in her native land. At merely twenty-four years of age, her audacious plans and unfaltering resolve were nothing short of inspirational."[8]

He went on to say that even though I faced seemingly insurmountable challenges, he believed I would spearhead an important movement because of my zeal and determination. Our conversation led him to document my return to Africa and the campaign against FGM.

I had never thought about a documentary about my mission or imagined an award-winning documentary director would want to embark on such a project. I was a twenty-four-year-old immigrant mother of three who was living in Atlanta when the project began. While I was a movie fan, watching documentaries was not what I did in my "spare" time. I had just started going public with interviews and the petition. I knew the power of social media, but I'd never considered a documentary as a medium to get out a message. I had no idea it could be such a vital advocacy tool.

In fact, I had no clue how a documentary was even made. Filming was a grueling marathon. Hours of sitting for interviews. A camera in my face constantly. Shooting in volatile situations. Retakes if there was any background noise. I do not know how reality television stars do it. There were days when the intensity and the emotional depths we were exploring pulled me further from my comfort zone than I had ever been and threatened to overwhelm me. To say it was invasive for me, my family, and my friends is a gross understatement. Despite the hurdles, Patrick was my pillar of support as we filmed in the United States and the Gambia.

Filming in the Gambia was particularly intense, as the crew traveled with me as I sought a meeting with President Jammeh and visited people and places to show others what it took to be an activist. In one scene, I talked about FGM with my father. At that time, he was a staunch supporter of FGM and child marriage. Both of us shared our beliefs in a deeply respectful way. I felt my father heard me. In fact, at the end of the interview, he was captured on film announcing that his own newborn child, a girl, would not undergo

FGM. As an Imam, he was criticized after the film premiered for allowing the filming of our conversation. I will always be thankful for his courage and love for me.

Patrick recalled that scene in the Ciné-ONU interview: "From a filmmaking perspective, it was crucial to approach this conversation with a lens that captured the raw emotions and the profound shifts in understanding that were unfolding before us. It was a delicate balancing act—ensuring the authenticity of the moment was preserved while also providing a lens that could potentially foster dialogue and change in communities entrenched in these traditions."

Several moments in the filming particularly stand out for me: talking with the woman who cut me, meeting with a group of village women to speak openly about FGM, and conversing with Imam Fatty, who was the head Imam under President Jammeh. My discussion with Imam Fatty was really not a discussion at all. For two hours, he lectured me, while I patiently listened. Then I asked a specific question about whether or not Islamic law required women to have FGM. Remember, at that time, women and men were convinced girls needed to be cut to be good Muslims. I was shocked when Imam Fatty said it was not a religious requirement. On film! We had a sound bite that would make a huge difference in our fight.

Jaha's Promise premiered at the Copenhagen International Film Festival (CPH:DOX) in March 2017. I walked the red carpet with Crown Princess Mary of Denmark, who then sat beside me in support. In addition to Patrick and Kate, I was surrounded by people dear to me: Haddy, Sait, and Mary Healy. My most cherished guest was my daughter, Khadija. I was dressed in a black princess gown by a Gambian designer, while she wore a Cinderella gown in white. Our outfits were so fitting because the whole occasion felt like a fairy tale.

The film was also screened at the United Nations, premiered in the United Kingdom at the Sheffield International Documentary Festival, and was shown at numerous other events and film festivals. It is now available on multiple streaming platforms. I do not know how many people have seen it, but it has led to some remarkable things.

My nomination for the Nobel Peace Prize was put forth by Jette Christensen, then a member of the Norwegian parliament, whom I met at a documentary film festival in Bergen, Norway. Meeting Jette Christensen, who saw *Jaha's Promise* at the festival, fostered a relationship that spurred community engagement across Norway. On the other side of the world, we at Safe Hands for Girls took our pink bus to villages throughout the Gambia to share the documentary. Equipped with a film projector at the back of the bus, we turned each screening of *Jaha's Promise* into a significant local event, complete with discussions.

The documentary has received numerous awards. At CPH:DOX 2017, the film was nominated for the F:ACT Award. It was nominated for the Sheffield Youth Jury Award at the Sheffield International Documentary Festival in 2017. And the film won the Audience Award at the GlobeDocs Film Festival in Boston.

One of the most important comments about the film was made during an NPR interview with Purna Sen, then the director of the policy division at UN Women. "Jaha's story shows how one woman can make a huge difference in breaking the silence surrounding female genital mutilation." This statement resonated with me for two reasons. First, it reaffirmed my belief that stories have power. They make things real and relevant. They make us act. Second, it proclaimed that one person can make a difference. While our power lies in the collective, recognizing the power of the individual is vital.

At its essence, the making of *Jaha's Promise* was about putting a face on the issue of FGM to drive change. It met that goal. Little did I know that my face would soon be used to advance the cause even further in a very unexpected way.

Chapter 15

Social Activism Meets Beauty

M Y FIRST EXPERIENCE MODELING was for the 2018 Pirelli Calendar, which has a cult following that looks forward to the calendar's release every year. This was the forty-fifth edition, shot by British fashion photographer Tim Walker. Eighteen people from the world of movies, music, and social activism posed for the calendar, the theme of which was *Alice in Wonderland*. We all felt excitement and pride because Tim had decided to portray a Black Alice with an entirely Black cast. I was particularly moved to be chosen because I was neither a model nor a celebrity.

When Tim reached out to me through a booking agency, I was surprised and happy he saw me as a strong woman who could contribute to this creative endeavor. The shoot spanned two long days, and I spent countless hours in the same outfit. The constant attention from the makeup and hair teams ensured every detail was perfect. While I enjoyed the beautification process, it was draining. But as with *Jaha's Promise* and my work with L'Oréal, I saw the calendar as an important way to put a face to issues nobody wanted to talk about. If people looked at that calendar and learned about my story, it was a win in the fight in which we were—and still are— engaged.

It was extraordinary to be in a global cast that included Naomi Campbell, the British supermodel and actress; Australian model Adut Akech; Ghanaian British fashion model and feminist activist Adwoa Aboah; Senegalese German model Alpha Dia; Beninese American actor and activist Djimon Hounsou; South Sudanese

Australian model Duckie Thot; British model King Owusu; American rapper and singer Lil Yachty; Kenyan Mexican actress Lupita Nyong'o; American actor, television personality, and singer-songwriter RuPaul; American actress Sasha Lane; American rapper, singer, songwriter, actor, record producer, and entrepreneur Sean "Diddy" Combs; American model Slick Woods; South African model and lawyer Thando Hopa; American actress, comedian, author, and television host Whoopi Goldberg; British model Wilson Oryema; and British fashion stylist, designer, and singer Zoe Bedeaux.

The Pirelli Calendar was my first modeling experience, but I had entered the world of beauty and fashion a few years earlier, when I was named a L'Oréal Paris Women of Worth honoree in 2015. This signature philanthropic program embodies the L'Oréal Paris belief that every woman is worth it. It elevates women who find beauty in giving back. I was and remain a big fan of L'Oréal, not only of their products but also of their message about women.

So, it was a truly magical moment for me when, five years later, I became the first Women of Worth honoree to be named a L'Oréal Paris global brand ambassador. Me, a girl who grew up in a small village in the Gambia, was now representing one of the most beloved brands in the beauty industry!

This honor came to me mainly because of Julien Calot, the chief creative officer at McCann Paris, a French advertising agency. McCann devised and launched the slogan "Because You're Worth It" for L'Oréal in 1973. Julien was responsible for L'Oréal's advertising. I met him at a Paris photo shoot, and we clicked instantly. He expressed his desire to have me become an international spokesperson for L'Oréal. Although the prospect was exciting, I tried not to get my hopes up too high. I was certainly not a celebrity like Beyoncé. I was a real woman combating FGM, a grim subject and worlds apart from the glamour of beauty brands. I found it surprising that the top beauty brand in the world wanted to associate with this cause.

Julien's proposal was supported by Delphine Viguier-Hovasse, global brand president of L'Oréal Paris and the first woman ever to take the helm of the French beauty giant's signature brand. Both of them both genuinely appreciated my work and the cause I championed. They wanted me to represent the L'Oréal brand despite the fact that I did not have the celebrity status of previous global brand ambassadors, like Beyoncé and Helen Mirren. They valued me as a real woman doing real work.

All of a sudden, I was in television and print ads. Participating in commercial shoots was quite an experience. I would spend entire days as the creatives aimed to get one perfect image or to shoot a minute-long commercial. One time, a group of the global ambassadors were gathered for a shoot at the Eiffel Tower. It was quite challenging for me due to my fear of heights and the cold weather, not to mention the fact that I was wearing high heels and stylish, but not necessarily warm, clothing.

I traveled globally, representing L'Oréal at events. I especially remember attending Paris Fashion Week. I felt like a celebrity, especially since I stayed at the same hotel as such famous personalities as Helen Mirren and Eva Longoria. People were constantly gathered outside the hotel, anticipating the appearance of the stars. Even though they might not have recognized me, the atmosphere was electrifying. I had not been exposed to many celebrities, but I did not feel intimidated by famous people. Their fame did not influence my opinion of them. In many cases, I became familiar with their work only after I met them and did a quick online search.

I saw these encounters as opportunities to promote awareness about FGM, and I used the public's curiosity about my identity to draw attention to the cause. L'Oréal's embrace offered me more than just a partnership; it provided a platform. Whenever I emerged from a hotel, curious eyes searching for celebrities like Camila Cabello would inadvertently land on me. The need to know who I was served my cause. The world would Google my name, and they would learn about FGM through me.

I love Paris deeply, the fashion, the food, and the charming streets. My first Paris Fashion Week was magical, and the magic was accentuated by the luxurious hotel stay, with amenities like twenty-four-hour room service. I even tried caviar for the first time. It was such a radical departure from my life in New York. My second Paris Fashion Week was with George, my third husband. It felt like a splendid vacation as we celebrated George's birthday on October 1, during that trip. It is a memory I will always cherish.

L'Oréal did not hand me just a contract; it also handed me confidence. It gave me a voice, a power, an ability to redefine my narrative. The effect was so profound that signing on with L'Oréal stands out as one of the most empowering moments in my life. It was not about the lucrative paychecks, even though they were helpful in terms of funding our activist efforts. It was about regaining control over my self-image.

While I was growing up, I was often reminded of my "oversized" eyes and chubby cheeks. Comparisons with my sisters' beauty overshadowed my self-worth. In a world laden with beauty standards, I had grown up feeling distinctly apart from what was perceived as beautiful. The physical attribute I did receive compliments about—from men—was my breasts, which made me feel like a sexual object. I am considered fairly light-skinned, a trait that is often unjustly favored. My skin tone has sometimes granted me privileges, including leadership opportunities during my school years. But I never truly felt beautiful, even when others told me I was. When L'Oréal embraced me and my face, it felt like an irrefutable stamp of approval. After that, no one could make me doubt my beauty.

One thing I love about being a L'Oréal spokesperson is the makeup. My beauty rituals have become my armor. I enjoy makeup for its ability to enhance one's natural beauty. I do not use it daily, but I appreciate the confidence and versatility it offers. I have grown to love my eyes. Now, with the right makeup, I can accentuate them beautifully. Depending on my mood, I like the variety of looks I can achieve with makeup, from bold to understated. I feel the best when I'm wearing bright, bold colors and lipstick. Unfortunately, I have also noticed there is a glaring lack of cosmetics catering to African skin tones. I admire L'Oréal's attempts to address this and would love to collaborate with them to develop a line specifically for African complexions.

As a L'Oréal global brand ambassador, I have had the opportunity to do interviews with magazines I love (just as much as the romance novels I read as a teen). I was featured in *Allure* and *Glamour.* That was heady stuff. Not exactly a Nobel Peace Prize nomination, but it did appeal to a young woman like me. The *Allure* interview made me realize the way I look and express myself through beauty products is my way of showing the world how strong I am. My past does not define me. I want to stand out, not fade into the background. I do not want people to see me as a victim and feel sorry for me.

Most importantly, being an international spokesperson has enabled me to connect with audiences I once thought were beyond my reach. Through L'Oréal, I can exhibit my pride in being a woman and inspire young African girls who've experienced hardships similar to mine to believe in their potential. L'Oréal changed everything.

I felt this very strongly when McCann Paris created a series of video testimonials called "Lessons of Worth" to amplify the meaning of L'Oréal's iconic tagline "Because You're Worth It" and underline the unwavering faith in women's power and intrinsic value. On International Women's Day in 2023, L'Oréal Paris released three new videos featuring international ambassadors: actress Elle Fanning, Brazilian model and activist Luma Grothe, and me. In our video testimonials, we talked authentically about being a woman— our path, our doubts, our fight against judgmental behaviors, and the importance of embracing self-worth. Here is what I said in mine:

> *I'm worth it.*
> *It should go without saying that those words are about*
> *the right of a woman,*
> *every woman,*

to choose what she does with her money,
what she does with her body, what she does with her life.

But here I am,
living, breathing proof that we are still not there. Yet.
And I don't know about you, but I'm getting impatient.

So I want you to come a little closer. And really listen to
  me. Look at me.
You see a woman who's been through fire.
You see a woman who was sent across the world and
  forced into a marriage with a man she'd never met,
whose body was mutilated before she was old enough to
  speak up and say no.
But look again.
You see a woman who has decided that is not the end of
  her story.
A woman who refuses to be a victim.
You see a woman who feels beautiful, and who feels
  stronger every single day.

You see a woman who enjoys makeup.
A woman who enjoys sex.
A woman with a platform.
A woman with a voice, determined to use it.
To speak up for those who can't.

You see a woman who runs her own business.
A woman who can choose to be the youngest female
  presidential candidate in the history of her country
  and do everything she can to ensure that her daugh-
  ter and your daughter and your granddaughter and
  her granddaughter

Never have to wonder
why some people still haven't figured it out yet.
So repeat after me.
I choose my life because I'm worth it.[9]

This mantra "I'm worth it" often provides the necessary fuel I need to continue the fight. Being an activist is exhausting and often bruises the heart and spirit in ways I cannot begin to convey. Unless one develops a core muscle that is built on self-love and confidence, the burden can simply become too much to bear, because the fight does not end. Small victories can bring even bigger setbacks. One girl saved does not ease the pain of another one lost.

I fight because I am worth it. I fight because women are worth it. I fight because children are worth it. I fight because all people are worth it.

Chapter 16

The Fight Continues

Since laws against FGM and child marriage in the Gambia have been enacted, my organization has intensified our efforts. Recent studies indicate advocacy efforts have reached an impressive 95 percent of people in the Gambia, denoting that most of the population is aware of the laws against FGM. This achievement underscores the importance of advocacy in educating and reaching the masses. We recognize the importance of laws as preventive tools but understand they alone cannot alter societal norms or mindsets. Our learning has guided us to pair legal efforts with education and to involve every sector of the community in our advocacy and educational projects.

We have focused on religious leaders. The issue of FGM has been easier to tackle with this group than child marriage. Historically, specific religious texts mention the Prophet's wife, Aisha, being married at a very young age. This has made it quite challenging to convince religious individuals that child marriage is wrong. Despite these hurdles, encouraging religious leaders to incorporate advocacy against these harmful practices in their Friday sermons and discussions with their congregations is crucial. We aim to enlighten them about the negative impacts of these practices and to emphasize the significance of education.

We have worked on building the capacity of religious leaders not just in the Gambia but also in other countries via collaboration with global organizations. For instance, I partnered with the World Bank as a consultant to conduct awareness-raising workshops

in Mauritania, where we brought together religious and traditional leaders from across Africa. Similarly, we collaborated with
UN Women to train traditional leaders in Zambia. I also had the
opportunity to work with the US State Department when organizing training sessions in Senegal with the participation of religious
leaders from various regions and nations, including West Africa and
Egypt. Our goal in these training programs is to nurture the development of religious leaders as agents of change, so that they then
are able to assist us in our advocacy initiatives. We aim to prevent
the misuse of the teachings of Islam or any other religion to justify
harmful practices.

Even while I was writing this memoir, the issues continued with
some religious leaders not resting in their efforts to oppose our cause.
For example, the former Imam of the State House Mosque, Abdou-
lie Fatty, whose declaration that FGM is not a religious requirement
was caught on film during the making of *Jaha's Promise*, called for
a social and economic boycott of all those campaigning against the
practice. He declared that Gambians concerned about their faith's
purity should not deal with anti-FGM campaigners, should stop
patronizing their businesses, and should avoid attending their weddings, naming ceremonies, and funerals.

According to Imam Fatty, FGM was recommended and accepted
in Islam, and anyone who denied that was a disbeliever. He cited
scholars and organizations that have ruled that female circumcision is an obligation for Muslim women. He also discredited Gam-
cotrap (the Gambia Committee on Traditional Practices Affecting
the Health of Women and Children), a long-standing and reputable
Gambian NGO, by calling on the committee to release a list of children who have died from FGM. Further actions on his part included
paying the fines of three women who were sentenced for carrying
out FGM and calling on Muslim youth associations in the country
to launch a petition campaign to repeal the 2015 amendment to the
Women's Act, which criminalized FGM.

I am appalled that Imam Fatty also tried to incite violence against people who are fighting against FGM. Islam does not advocate violence between people who have different viewpoints on an issue. We are not fighting against the *Sunnah*, as Imam Fatty said. In Islam, *Sunnah* refers to the traditions and practices of the Prophet Muhammad, and it constitutes a model for Muslims to follow. Imam Fatty's argument was a rehash of an old false belief that I and others who are anti-FGM are fighting against Islam. I love my religion deeply.

Furthermore, some Muslim countries, such as Dubai, Qatar, and Saudi Arabia, do not practice FGM. Saudi is the capital of the Islamic world, and their daughters do not go through FGM, as it is illegal in that country. Al-Azhar University in Egypt, the chief center of Islamic and Arabic learning in the world, does not deal with FGM, because it has nothing to do with Islam.

In light of Imam Fatty's attack, I asked anyone using Islam to continue pushing this agenda to silence anti-FGM campaigners to sit down with us and have a conversation, because it is not us against them. We are not enemies, and we are all Gambians.

One argument currently being made in the effort to remove the ban on FGM is that rather than legislating against FGM, the medicalization of the practice should be promoted. Proponents advocate setting up private clinics where girls and women would go to be cut and to receive medical treatment if they got an infection or experienced high levels of bleeding, both of which can lead to death. As of this writing, Egypt has these clinics, and the Gambia and Liberia are considering setting them up.

My own view is we are significantly lacking evidence that allowing FGM under these conditions is good practice. We simply do not have good research on the physical, emotional, and psychological consequences of FGM. Additionally, the arguments against FGM are not just health related. FGM takes away choice from young girls and women who are not in the position to make informed decisions. FGM constitutes a male-dominated view of what a woman's sexuality should be and how her body should look. FGM should be a women's issue, not one whose fate is determined by male religious and political leaders to suit their own agendas. What we do know without a doubt is that FGM is not a prerequisite for being a good Muslim.

Additionally, I worry about access to these clinics if they are set up. For instance, how will poor people get the money needed to travel to clinics from rural locations? Even if they are able, the most important question is, how can women who are fighting for their survival every day not be protected when it comes to their own bodies? The pressure on them is already immense. Do we need to add more hardship to their lives with FGM practices? And how will our youth react to the reinstatement of FGM as a legitimate procedure? Is that what they want for their future?

I think the better option is education, and that is what we have been focused on. Safe Hands has been developing youth programs in the Gambia by utilizing the network of school clubs across the country. It is vital for young individuals to comprehend their rights and for us to integrate reproductive-health education into our educational systems. We have also been collaborating with the Ministry of Education and other governmental agencies to include campaigns against FGM and child marriage in their health programs.

After the laws against FGM and child marriage were enacted in the Gambia, we also initiated training programs with the Gambian military and police to foster a broader understanding of FGM and child marriage issues. We developed a program where all recruits into the police force and the national army underwent gender training to understand FGM and child marriage. This was essential because the legislation would only be effective if those responsible for its enforcement believed in it and supported it.

Recently, we have been exploring sports, mainly soccer, as a medium by which to educate young men. This approach stems from the major influence of soccer in the Gambia. In the past, we engaged in various activities, such as organizing soccer matches, to raise awareness regarding FGM and child marriages. We distributed educational materials, spoke before the start of tournaments, and even sponsored some events. These actions were not typical development initiatives, but we carried them out to build trust, connect with the hearts and minds of people, and encourage them to listen to our message. Finding resources remains a significant challenge in our efforts: the lack of support or understanding from potential backers sometimes hinders the implementation of effective strategies.

Outside of the Gambia, we have initiated campaigns to influence legislation in other African countries where FGM and child marriage are still prevalent. For example, in Liberia, Sierra Leone, and Mali, we have been pushing for the implementation of laws criminalizing FGM. In Liberia I have collaborated with traditional leaders, UN Women (in my role as a Goodwill Ambassador), lawmakers, government ministries, including the Ministry of Gender, Children and Social Protection, and the Liberian government to foster understanding and promote the establishment of these necessary laws.

In many countries, working with traditional leaders is an intricate undertaking, given their deeply rooted beliefs and practices, which sometimes seem at odds with development protocols. For instance, they may observe rituals involving ancestral appeasement that are crucial in their decision-making process. Explaining these complexities to funding organizations that expect conventional accounting for expenses is often challenging. We must navigate the intricate cultural terrain with a focus on long-term impacts and make concessions for cultural and traditional nuances if we are to be genuinely committed to eradicating FGM. It is also crucial to acknowledge all parties involved in these undertakings to ensure inclusivity and recognition for their efforts, thereby fostering a community-wide approach to addressing these issues.

One effort I am very proud of is the Big Sisters Movement (BSM), which was launched on International Women's Day in 2018. We are the largest grassroots coalition of local NGOs led by women survivors of FGM and child marriage from Nigeria, the Gambia, Sierra Leone, Kenya, and Somalia. Our goal is to enable survivors to tell their stories, advocate, and find grassroots solutions in Africa. The Big Sister Movement has yet to become what I want it to be due to a lack of funding, but it is something I am working toward. I aim to turn BSM into the most significant survivor- and Africa-led movement, one by us and for us. I want it to consider all our struggles and challenges, including the ones traditional funding organizations have failed to understand.

During the announcement of our coalition, I said, "For too long, international organizations have been leading the campaign in Africa, implementing programs together with local activists in our communities. The time has come for Africans across the Continent and the world to be at the forefront of the campaign to end female genital mutilation and early child marriage in Africa by 2030. African women tend to be perceived as women who need to be saved. They are never considered as the actual saviors."

While our work is centralized in Africa, I must emphasize that FGM and child marriages are global issues. In the 1950s even *Playboy* magazine promoted female circumcision in the United States, illustrating this is not an issue confined to Africa. FGM is reported in various countries outside Africa, including Malaysia, the Maldives, and Colombia. Due to the diverse immigrant population in the United States, FGM is also occurring there, and the same is true for France. This issue affects over two hundred million women around the globe, with many more unaccounted for. The problem transcends borders and ethnic backgrounds, affecting individuals in communities worldwide.

Furthermore, the exploitation of young girls, driven by an unhealthy fascination with their bodies, is a global issue. As a result, many people, including some educated African women, seek to minimize FGM by comparing FGM to cosmetic procedures like labiaplasty, whereby women alter their genitalia to conform to standards often set by pornography and other industries. The notion that young girls are desirable sexual beings is a global narrative fueled by various interest groups. These industries, and factors like poverty and a lack of education, exacerbate the problem, pushing young girls into vulnerable situations where they are exploited further.

Acknowledging and addressing these global dimensions as we continue our efforts to eradicate FGM and child marriages is imperative. I am trusting young leaders worldwide—and particularly in Africa—to take on these issues. I believe the future rests in their hands.

Chapter 17

Developing Young Leaders

IN AFRICA WE PROUDLY CLAIM the title of the continent with the youngest population of any around the globe. In fact, 70 percent of those residing in sub-Saharan Africa are under thirty. These young people stand as a living testament to our continent's potential to blossom and evolve. I wholeheartedly believe in embracing the zest and creativity these young minds bring to the table. Integrating them actively into the arenas of decision-making and innovation is not just about promoting inclusivity. It is also about forming a vital cornerstone in our blueprint for fostering continuous economic growth, igniting innovation, and safeguarding peace and security in Africa.

This is not just about supporting young activists; it is also about developing young leaders. It starts with acknowledging the importance of developing community among us. I know this because of the supportive communities I have been honored to be a part of. I constantly advise young leaders to become active in groups that will help them develop their skills and connections and will provide them with sustenance.

My first significant interaction with fellow young activists outside of the Gambia and the United States was in a weeklong meeting in Kenya organized by *The Guardian*. I met young people like me who were working tirelessly toward eradicating FGM. I felt immense joy and camaraderie when I met individuals like Domtila Chesang, a Kenyan women's rights activist and the founder of I_ Rep Foundation, which seeks to eradicate FGM and child marriage, works to improve girls' access to education, and addresses violence against girls and women. Meeting other young Africans who shared the same sentiments and passion for the cause was incredibly comforting. This meeting helped me realize I was not an isolated figure in this fight.

The camaraderie extended beyond just me and my team and involved a network of like-minded individuals who were equally passionate. Our time in Kenya was filled with various activities, such as singing, dancing, and strategizing ways to combat FGM. It fostered strong connections among us, culminating in the creation of a WhatsApp group and channels of communication through other social media platforms. This network remains active to this day, providing a platform for continuous collaboration and the sharing of ideas. We have fostered a community where everyone feels supported and valued.

This coming together of young activists is so important because sometimes our struggle leads to competition for resources, causing fragmentation within the movement, infighting, and negativity. Unfortunately, this competition is not unique to the FGM space. Still, it is a pervasive issue across various sectors on the continent. I believe we must work toward changing this dynamic. The aim should not be competition, as there is ample space for everyone to contribute toward the common goal. It is also necessary to address the role of development partners, who sometimes inadvertently foster competition by pitting groups against each other. I will share some thoughts on this later in the book.

Personally, I work hard not to get involved in any of this drama and to quietly foster collaboration instead. People often regard me as a respected figure, sometimes referring to me as a big sister or even "Ma." This respect is not necessarily tied to age but rather to the work I do. I tap into that respect so that it serves as a unifying force in this space, fostering learning and healing. Additionally, our work significantly affects us psychologically, necessitating a focus on healing and self-care. I envision organizing retreats that serve as safe spaces for activists to rejuvenate, share experiences, and uplift each other, fostering a sense of community rather than a battleground.

Uniting young leaders involves more than just working in the nonprofit and development sectors. It is also about working in politics. I was nominated to be the co-chair of the Youth Inter-Party Committee of the Gambia. This nomination represented the most significant opportunity I had at the time to serve and give back to my country. It was a vote of confidence from all the Gambia's political parties to serve at such a crucial stage in our history. I was deeply honored.

However, this co-chair post created a dilemma since I had also taken on the role of managing co-founder of the campaign Until We Are Equal, spearheaded by Resist This Pac. This initiative was blossoming under the remarkable guidance of my friend Xander Schultz, an entrepreneur, social justice investor, and activist who has worked assiduously to empower vulnerable groups in and outside the United States. Through this campaign, we aimed to propel the progressive movement forward by aiding marginalized communities and their leaders in building unparalleled power. Our primary focus was to amplify the political influence of women in the United States by substantially supporting organizations piloted by Black and Brown women.

Initially, I was worried that my role in Until We Are Equal would prevent me from engaging actively in Gambian politics. I recall a conversation I had with Xander after I realized I had forgotten to inform him of my travels. When he inquired about my whereabouts, I hesitantly said, "Gambia." His response illustrated his belief in my vision and showcased his genuine investment in my growth. He commended my dedication and assured me that my contributions to the Gambia would not be stifled. I am sharing this experience because it shows that support fosters growth in young leaders. I am immensely grateful to Xander for allowing me to serve meaningfully without compromising my integrity. His faith in me came at a time when I needed it most. Regrettably, my formal involvement with Until We Are Equal ended when I had to travel extensively in the Gambia during the election period.

The NewNow is another significant initiative I have been involved with that supports young leaders. This initiative brings together individuals from diverse backgrounds, selected based on their contributions to various sectors. The initiative has been especially important in providing a support system for young leaders navigating complex leadership paths. It fosters deep connections and lifelong friendships among members, providing a support network that assists them in finding solutions to problems, even when operating in different sectors.

One poignant example of this support network's effectiveness was provided during a recent crisis in Afghanistan. Members collaborated to help evacuate the family of one of our colleagues, Roya, from Afghanistan, showcasing the solidarity and unity within the group. This experience highlighted the importance of having a network of individuals willing to step up and assist during times of crisis. Support goes beyond monetary contributions, and it fosters a deep sense of friendship, family, and camaraderie.

Regarding its funding, it is worth noting that the NewNow continues to be funded by Virgin Unite and Richard Branson, who played a significant role in bringing the initiative's leaders together. However, Richard has not assumed a formal title and allows the members to lead the initiative.

In addition to peer groups, mentorships are essential in the development of young leaders. I had the opportunity to be a part of the African Women Leaders Network (AWLN). The AWLN serves as a platform for intergenerational learning, allowing younger members like me to learn from the experiences of older women who had paved the way in various sectors of society. By fostering a cycle of learning and mentorship that is beneficial for all members, the AWN provides a rich environment for personal and professional development. Its notable members include former presidents Ellen

Johnson Sirleaf of Liberia, Joyce Banda of Malawi, and Ameenah Gurib-Fakim of Mauritius. During my time with AWLN, I received valuable advice from women in the group. In particular, Phumzile Mlambo-Ngcuka, the executive director of UN Women, was an important mentor for me, offering guidance and support.

I particularly love working closely and sharing leadership skills with other women. My friend Aya Chebbi, former youth envoy for the African Union, founded the Nala Feminist Collective, a Pan-African group of seventeen feminists on a mission to enable, foster, and mobilize young women from Africa and the diaspora. The name *Nala* is of Swahili origin and means "a successful person who achieves everything." This group has helped me connect with and develop meaningful friendships with women leaders, such as Bogolo Kenewendo, a global economist with vast expertise in international trade and development.

Apart from my engagement with formal organizations geared toward supporting young leaders, I have always been passionate about nurturing young leaders in my midst. This passion has led me to initiate various personal projects to develop young leaders in various capacities. I often employ young individuals or allow them to volunteer at my organization. This provides them with valuable field experience and allows me to engage in mentorship, as I can share insights and the realities of our work with them.

Furthermore, I actively mentor young leaders, offering guidance and advice based on my experiences, through various platforms, including social media networks like Snapchat. Maintaining an open line of communication with a global community of young individuals who look up to me for guidance and advice has been gratifying. Through these interactions, I nurture their aspirations and guide them in their journeys, thereby fostering a community of future leaders well equipped to take on the challenges of tomorrow.

I have been honored to have numerous mentees whom I guide and empower, ensuring they avoid repeating the mistakes I made. Honesty is at the core of my mentorship, as I believe in sharing the realities of being a changemaker and helping them recognize their true worth. Whether it is navigating the complexities of international development agencies or empowering them to negotiate for fair treatment, I am dedicated to equipping them with the tools they need to succeed.

In recent times, I have witnessed firsthand the transformative power of social media in activism, particularly when it involves potential young leaders. Its influence is as vast as it is unpredictable. You never quite know who will come across your message and how it might alter their perspective or actions. I recall a profound conversation that deterred an individual from subjecting their daughter to FGM. This kind of deep, meaningful interaction is now possible on a much larger scale, thanks to the networks social media fosters.

I have established a presence on various platforms, each of which offers a unique way to engage with different audiences. Instagram allows for a rich visual representation of narratives, while Twitter facilitates quick yet profound exchanges of ideas. Recently, I embarked on a journey through TikTok, a space that merges creativity with information dissemination, and Snapchat, a platform I frequent daily for its lively personal chat features.

My approach to social media is twofold. It is a powerful tool in my advocacy efforts against FGM and child bias, since it fosters spaces where vital discussions and debates occur. Simultaneously, it has become a nurturing ground for young leaders and activists. It is a hub where they can connect, learn, and grow together, and thus it is spearheading a new generation of empathetic and informed leaders.

Initially, I tried to keep my virtual engagements separate from my real-world interactions. However, recent events and encounters have gradually blurred these boundaries. Friendships nurtured online have blossomed into genuine, enriching relationships, forming a supportive network in my personal and professional life.

When it comes to leadership development in activism, I emphasize nurturing specific traits in budding leaders: honesty, courage, integrity, and a deep-seated love for the community they aspire to serve. I advocate for a quieter resolve, which sometimes speaks louder than vociferous protests. A level of calmness and understanding enables young leaders to steer heated discussions gracefully and show empathy and compassion even in the face of disagreement.

This journey has not just been about fostering growth in others; it has been a path of personal evolution, as well. Over the years, I have grown more empathetic and understanding, a transformation that has heightened my effectiveness as an activist. Enriched by an increasing number of interactions and a deeper understanding of various communities and their unique challenges, I have embraced a broader perspective.

My strategy in activism leans more toward instinct rather than meticulously structured plans. My role in this domain is a life's mission, a path carved out for me by a higher power. This profound belief in my purpose propels me forward, allows me to navigate situations and environments with an intuitive understanding. It is about reading the room, understanding the undercurrents, and reacting based on a deep-seated intuition honed over years of experience.

As I forge ahead and continue to evolve and adapt as a leader in the activism sphere, I remain committed to nurturing connections and championing vital causes. I am dedicated to cultivating a community—a village—grounded in love and compassion.

Chapter 18

It Takes a Village

THE PHRASE "IT TAKES A VILLAGE to raise a child" originates from an African proverb and conveys the message that it takes many people ("a village") to provide a safe, healthy environment for children, one where children are given the security they need to develop and flourish and realize their hopes and dreams.

It also takes a village to be an activist. In my journey, I have been blessed with the presence of advocates and mentors, who have significantly impacted my life and work. Without my children, family, and friends, I would not have had the love needed to go through such difficult times. These individuals have become pillars of support, guiding me through challenges and empowering me to strive for change. In addition, there are so many people and organizations throughout the years who have fought valiantly to help create a better world. All my work rests on the shoulders of these courageous individuals.

The truth is that for everyone—not just activists—the journey through life can be solitary, filled with moments of loneliness and uncertainty. During these times, the presence of true friends becomes a beacon of light, reminding us of our worth and providing the unwavering support we so desperately need. I have come to realize we cannot navigate the complexities of life alone; we need the companionship and encouragement of those who believe in us and uplift our spirits.

The roles of an advocate and a mentor are intertwined and deeply personal. A mentor is not only someone who believes in their mentee but also someone who champions their cause. Mentors guide us through the twists and turns of life, imparting wisdom and sharing their own experiences. They become our protectors, shielding us from hardships and adversity. There are so many out there. Throughout my career, I've been blessed with an incredible support system. I would not be where I am today without the countless individuals who believed in me and stood by me. While it is impossible to name everyone, I must express my immense gratitude to those who have shared my vision. Some I have already introduced you to, but I want to share more details about them, along with naming others who have impacted my story.

I cannot say enough about Taina Bien-Aimé; she is my hero and a mother figure who saved me when I needed it most as a lost teenager in New York City. Taina embodies love and kindness, and she instilled in me a belief in my worth and the power of my light to change the world. Even when I doubted myself, her confidence in me did not waver. She has been instrumental in my growth. Taina introduced me to the works of Maya Angelou and Haitian writers, sparking my love for reading and enhancing my English skills. Her belief in my voice and my potential has been a constant source of inspiration, making her a vital part of my life.

Alhagie Manka, a filmmaker I met early in my career, has become family to me. He fights for me like no one else, going above and beyond to support and protect me. He has documented my work extensively and knows my story and my vision more intimately than anyone else. He is an advisor and mediator, providing honest feedback and helping me navigate challenges. He is a father figure to my children and a rock of support in my life. I cherish our deep friendship and the way he pours his heart into everything he does.

Sait Matty Jaw was instrumental in helping us launch a youth movement against FGM in the Gambia. He is a co-founder and the executive director of the Center for Research and Policy Development (CRPD), an independent, nonprofit, and nonpartisan social research, advocacy, learning, and capacity-building organization committed to promoting inclusive democratic governance in the Gambia. He is exceptionally passionate about our country and its youth. I regard Sait as a brother and have immense respect for him. If there is anyone I would choose to lead the Gambia, it would be Sait, even ahead of myself. He consistently exudes positivity, always seeking solutions rather than focusing on problems. Sait refrains from interpreting actions in a negative light, an admirable trait that never ceases to amaze me. Without his presence and drive, we would not have achieved what we have.

An unlikely friendship blossomed between Richard Branson and me, and it has profoundly impacted what I do professionally and personally. From the moment we met, there was an instant connection. He and his charitable arm, Virgin Unite, led by the extraordinary president Jean Olewang, have been incredible advocates of our work. A visionary, business magnate, and philanthropist, Richard possesses such humility and humanity, and this has left a lasting impression on me. Whenever I find myself in trouble or on the brink of giving up, he and his organization extend a helping hand in various ways. Whether offering financial assistance during challenging times or inviting me into a circle of remarkable leaders, he and Virgin Unite remind me that I am not alone in my struggles.

I vividly recall a life-changing moment when Richard took me to the Apartheid Museum in Johannesburg, South Africa. Tears streamed down my face in the presence of the stories of Nelson Mandela and the freedom fighters, who sacrificed so much. It was a profound awakening and a stark reminder of the sacrifices made.

Nimco Ali, a force to be reckoned with, has shown me the power of standing in my truth. She is a British social activist of Somali heritage and the co-founder and CEO of the Five Foundation, a global partnership to end female genital mutilation. Nimco's authenticity and unwavering commitment to our cause inspire me. She has been there for me during life's highs and lows, offering guidance and support. Our friendship is built on trust and understanding, and I am grateful for her presence in my life.

Xander Schultz has become a trusted confidant and advocate. He is an entrepreneur, a social impact investor, and an activist who is focused on maximizing the freedom of oppressed people and elevating changemakers. Xander connects people and endeavors to help wherever he can. Our bond is strong, and his guidance and friendship continue to uplift and inspire me.

Abdalaziz Alhamza's remarkable journey as a Syrian journalist and human rights defender is awe-inspiring. His resilience and ability to find joy even in the face of adversity are qualities I deeply admire. He has been a constant source of support and has stood by my side through thick and thin. Our friendship brings laughter, mischief, and is based on a profound understanding of each other's experiences.

Maggie O'Kane, a foreign correspondent with *The Guardian*, was deeply passionate about eradicating FGM. Despite the professional risks, she advocated to promote our campaign to end FGM. I am grateful for *The Guardian*'s involvement, as it brought unprecedented awareness to the cause and thus contributed to a substantial decrease in FGM practices across Africa.

Susan Gibbs and Mary Healy were the first primary donors to Safe Hands for Girls. Through the Wallace Global Fund and Human Dignity Foundation, they offered critical support that allowed us to do our work in the most authentic way. They believed in our vision and stood by us when many funders did not understand our mission.

My Safe Hands team members are not just staff; I consider them my family. Our office abounds with unity and camaraderie, a testament to the harmonious personalities that converge here. Admittedly, many find my ideas audacious, but a spirit of innovation drives us. The dedication of my team is unparalleled—even in challenging times, such as when salaries are delayed, their commitment remains unwavering. Working with us is not merely doing a job; it's engaging in a passionate endeavor. With this formidable team, I've achieved all that I have.

The friendships I have fostered within the global networking community are as incredibly diverse as the people brought together by a shared passion for making a positive impact. Many of these connections were borne out of conferences, like the annual One Young World Summit, and were forged through Richard Branson's influential network. We support one another's endeavors and share memorable moments. While our causes and passions may vary, our shared commitment to effecting change and improving the world unites us.

Friendships within the activist community often emerge from a shared cause, but they go beyond that. The bonds we form through conferences, events, and collaborations deepen as we discover our collective dedication to making a difference. These friendships do not revolve solely around our shared activism. They also spring from genuine connections with individuals who possess a deep love for our world, a genuine devotion to their work, and an unwavering commitment to humanity. It is through these shared values and a profound connection with fellow human beings that true friendships blossom.

In the early years of my life, my social circle was confined to the people in my village and my immediate family. However, the digital world has opened doors to friendships that transcend physical boundaries. Surprisingly, some of these virtual friendships have become as meaningful and profound as my relationships with my family. They provide a different kind of support and create a sense of belonging and understanding that complements my in-person friendships.

One person I met online is Sana Sarr. He was one of the only Gambian men to stand up for me and others who were speaking out against FGM. Sana gave me advice and courage during my most challenging days and nights. He was also wonderfully funny. When I would be at a low point, Sana would message me out of the blue and say something stupid that would always make me laugh. He was always there for me and even came up with the name of our nonprofit.

I deeply value long-term relationships that embody the qualities of loyalty, honesty, and a shared sense of humor. I value family and friends who have stood by my side through my life's triumphs and trials. Laughter is vital in our relationships, as we find joy in shared moments of silliness. Whether dancing the night away, enjoying a meal together, or embarking on adventures, we create safe spaces where we can indeed be ourselves, surrounded by acceptance and love.

When I first came to New York City, one man whom I shall not name to protect his privacy, gained a special place in my heart, which he still holds as a dear friend. He and his parents have been there for me through thick and thin, offering unwavering support without judgment. His commitment to education inspired me to pursue my academic journey, and he continues to inspire me in countless ways. He is not just a friend; he is family.

Sometimes, individuals in our shared village have a falling-out. Two women who were childhood friends of mine and were instrumental in everything I accomplished are now estranged from me. Most of the fault lies with me, and I am working hard to make amends. One I will not name, but the other I will.

This unnamed woman is the definition of *feminism* in the Gambia; I deeply admire her courage and fearlessness and her ability to write and articulate things in such a powerful way. She was one of my biggest inspirations early in my activism and supported me immensely. Without her, I would not be where I am today or have even started. She and I are very different in the sense that I am not technical at all. I have visions and things I want to do, and she could write and explain them perfectly. She developed resentment toward me. When the media started covering our campaign, they focused mainly on me, which fueled resentment and grudges on her part and that of others in our group.

We experienced a conflict because others told me she had

spoken negatively about me. This situation strained our relationship. Reflecting upon it now, I realize I should have approached the problem differently. At the time, I was immature and often reacted impulsively to what others said and did to me. While I was young at the time, I cannot attribute my actions solely to my age. Recalling this individual's profound influence on my personal growth and recognizing her role in shaping who I am today, I should have given her the benefit of the doubt. Instead of distancing myself and engaging in an online dispute, which I initially blamed solely on her, I now understand I contributed significantly to the escalation of the conflict.

My childhood friend Haddy has constantly been present in my life. When I started my organization and began traveling extensively, Haddy was right there by my side. Even when I had my children with me, she would travel with us to various destinations across the world. However, our friendship faced its biggest challenge during my third marriage, to the man who had captured my heart. I was torn between my love for George and my loyalty to Haddy and our long-term friendship. I chose my husband.

Mine is not an unusual story. I know too many women who chose love for a man over loyalty to a best friend. My break with Haddy has been marked by loneliness and isolation. Losing the closeness has left a void in my life, and I miss having someone there who truly understands me, knows my deepest struggles, and stands by me through thick and thin. I will share more of our story in the next chapter.

Writing this memoir had me thinking a great deal about the relationships in my life because, at its essence, that is what being human is all about. As I reflect upon my journey, I find it surprising how deeply I've come to value the friendships, mentors, and advocates I've gained. By nature, I lean toward being introverted often preferring solitude or the familiar comfort of my thoughts. This trait surprises people, especially given the breadth of exceptional individuals I've connected with over the years.

I realize that friendships are not about being gregarious or constantly social but about the depth and genuine understanding I share with those I choose to let in. With each passing year, I have come to recognize my nature does not diminish the profound importance of these relationships in my life. They stand as a testament to the fact that even those of us who lean toward solitude can forge bonds that are as meaningful and strong as any. It is what makes us human.

HUMAN

Being human feels like a constant dance of light and shadow. It is about navigating the fragile balance of vulnerability and strength, of instinctual trust and learned caution. There is a deep emotional tapestry woven into our very essence, pulling at the heartstrings of our shared existence.

When I connect with others, it is like touching a part of the universe that is both vast and intimate. It is this inexplicable pull that makes me believe, perhaps naively, in the innate goodness of a stranger. But the pitfalls of such trust serve as heart-wrenching reminders of our limitations, of the ways our heart can mislead us, even with the best intentions.

Feelings run deep in the human experience. Even when we wear masks of resilience or indifference, there is a tidal wave of emotions beneath the surface, waiting to be acknowledged. Our silent battles, the echoes of criticisms, and the haunting memories are not mere fleeting thoughts but profound moments that shape our essence.

Yet amidst this complex emotional landscape are pockets of pure, unadulterated solace. For me, it is the embrace of nature—the hypnotic lull of waves at the beach or the tranquility of vast open spaces. They act as a balm, healing the frayed edges of a weary heart, grounding me when the world threatens to become too overwhelming.

Chapter 19

Love Found and Lost

I FIND IT FASCINATING THAT SOME of the details of my life seem coated with an opaque film, while others are so fresh and clear, I feel like I am still there. The love and loss of the only man I have ever truly loved is one of those experiences that remains so vivid in my mind. Perhaps it is because it was what truly sent me on the path of finding out what it means to be human.

I met George in 2021, when I was thirty-one. For the first time in my life, I experienced the sensation of falling in love, which I had only ever read about in teenage romance novels. In the Gambia, those novels were the closest I came to understanding what love should feel like. Romantic love and pleasure are not a part of my Gambian culture. Having lived through two child marriages by the time I was seventeen did not leave any room for fantasy. With George, I was not only a survivor and an activist; I felt like a woman, which was extraordinary. Until it was not.

I was sitting in my Gambian office one day, and my assistant approached me excitedly and cautiously. She had something to share, but she was worried about my reaction, knowing well my reservations about dating, especially when it came to Gambian men. Life experiences and the fear of judgment from my community had made me wary of putting myself out there romantically. But curiosity got the better of me, and I urged her to share her secret.

She told me about a man who had asked her persistently to introduce us, someone who had been searching for a connection with me for quite some time. She told me he was a businessman and was primarily focused on real estate. I knew if I was ever going to get involved with someone again, I needed a man who respected my work. She assured me he followed my achievements closely and admired my endeavors.

My curiosity was piqued even further when she told me he came from a highly respected family and when she described him as one of the most decent people she knew. He had helped her personally with her own spirituality. Her mention of this left an impression on me. As someone who values spirituality, it was one of the first qualities I sought in a partner. Perhaps it was my father's influence, but I yearned for a man who believed in God and could guide and support me on my spiritual journey. My faith is a cherished part of my life, and I wanted a partner who was even more spiritually inclined than I was. According to my assistant, George had those qualities. Of course, it did not hurt when she pulled up his picture. I could not help but think, *Well, he is good-looking.*

Feeling cautiously optimistic, I permitted her to give out my number *after* she asked him more questions to ensure we shared common values and interests. Later that day, I received a text from George. He jokingly mentioned the rigorous screening process my assistant had put him through before giving him my number. We shared details about our lives, where we were, and what we sought. This was customary for Gambians and especially for people from similar backgrounds, like us. I wanted to delve deeper into our compatibility, so I shared with him a link to the Love Language Quiz. ™ This quiz and the concept of the five love languages were developed by author and marriage counselor Gary Chapman to explain the five general ways romantic partners express and experience love. They are acts of service, receiving gifts, physical touch, quality time, and words of affirmation.

As we continued talking, we both took the quiz and exchanged results, initiating a meaningful discussion about our love languages. My highest score was in words of affirmation (30 percent), closely followed by physical touch (23 percent). I scored 17 percent on both quality time and acts of service, while my receiving gifts score ranked the lowest (13 percent). Being a natural giver, I had learned not to expect much from others. On the other hand, George's highest score was for quality time (32 percent), followed by acts of service (29 percent). He scored 19 percent on physical touch, 13 percent on words of affirmation, and at 6 percent on receiving gifts, his lowest score. Our Love Language Quiz™ results gave us a better understanding of ourselves and each other. We discussed the results and decided they accurately represented our needs and preferences.

As our conversations continued, I wanted to gain an even deeper understanding of George and myself. It was an unexpected step for me, as I had never been one to take personality tests; however, this time felt different. I wanted to make sure that I was not wasting my time and that this connection was worth pursuing. So, we both took the Myers-Briggs personality test, which indicates a person's core personality type based on how she or he perceives the world and makes decisions. It revealed fascinating insights into our characters. I emerged as an ESFP (Extroverted, Sensing, Feeling, and Perceiving). This personality type makes up only 6 percent of the population and is called the "entertainer." It describes a person who is spontaneous, resourceful, and outgoing. George came out as an INFP (Introversion, Intuition, Feeling, Perception). The rarest personality type, an INFP is a "mediator" and is quiet, open-minded, and imaginative. We certainly had our differences, but I thought they might make us complementary.

Our first call lasted a remarkable five hours. He was in Scotland, and I was in the Gambia. Yet the geographical distance dissolved as we immersed ourselves in each other's thoughts and feelings. After I hung up, I could not stop thinking about him. I knew it was just one call, but something about it had felt different. I was intrigued by the thought of exploring a potential relationship with someone who admired my work, shared similar values, and had a strong sense of spirituality. For the first time in my life, I felt giddy. Although I approached this with cautious optimism, I could not deny the excitement slowly building within me. Perhaps, just maybe, this could be the start of something beautiful.

Our connection felt profound and natural. He possessed a deep spirituality and shared many traits with my father, which drew me in. We found ease in our communication and understood each other effortlessly. Our interests aligned closely, with our movie and TV series preferences almost mirroring one another. Though I was not initially inclined toward philosophy and ancient philosophers, I found myself fascinated by George's views and perspectives on the topic. Men asked me out regularly, but this was the first time someone had really intrigued me.

From the beginning, we recognized our values regarding family and the qualities we sought in a spouse were aligned. It was an affirmation of our feelings for each other, and we quickly realized this was no ordinary relationship. In fact, we were both thinking about marriage before even meeting in person. It felt like he was the person I had been waiting for all my life.

Hours would fly by as we immersed ourselves in phone calls, and sometimes we opted for video calls. I remember seeing him on the screen, and the desire to be physically close to him often overwhelmed me. Was this what it felt like to fall in love? He read to me, and his voice was soothing and comforting. He was an avid gym goer, and occasionally, he would call me during his workout, and his breath would punctuate our conversation.

George learned I loved flowers, and to my surprise and delight, he sent money to my assistant so that she would buy me fresh flowers every day and bring them to work. It was a thoughtful gesture that filled me with joy. More than the flowers was George's genuine interest in me—all of me. The feelings I was developing for him left me satisfied.

I could feel myself falling, and it was as though fate had brought us together. Our virtual courtship was unconventional, but it felt right. Every conversation, every shared moment, and every gift of flowers was another step toward a love that felt destined, not arranged. Then he sent me a sweet message, expressing that he had dreamt of me and thought of me throughout the night. It warmed my heart, and I replied, telling him the feeling was mutual and I eagerly anticipated meeting him and possibly spending forever together. It was a bold statement, but it felt right.

An inexplicable familiarity with George resonated with me, even though we had not met in person yet. I would daydream about what it would be like to share my life with him. George's ambition and hard work struck me profoundly. He had accomplished so much for someone his age, owned various properties, and headed real estate projects. It was inspiring, and we were well matched in terms of our energy and aspirations.

His spiritual side appealed to me and played a significant role in shaping my thinking. He was a Sufi, and so he was following a different path from that of adherents to the Wahhabi Islamic tradition, which I had been exposed to in my early years. Our discussions about religion, philosophy, and God became the foundation of our relationship, and our shared curiosity allowed us to explore various perspectives and teachings. In my journey to comprehend religion better, I delved into books by Islamic scholars and saints. This exploration exposed me to a broader range of perspectives within Islam, and this led me to appreciate its teachings, morals, and emphasis on justice and peace.

George introduced me to tariqas, which are spiritual paths within Islam. Initially, I believed that following tariqas was not in line with actual Islamic teachings. Still, I realized the value of belonging to a community that offered support and understanding. George's influence challenged my prior beliefs and made me embrace a more holistic view of Islam.

During one call, he may have accidentally uttered those three magical words "I love you" under his breath as we said goodbye. My heart skipped a beat, and although he quickly hung up the phone, I texted him to acknowledge I heard what he said. His response was humble, as if he was trying to gauge my reaction, and

I reassured him I was falling for him. My excitement rose when he revealed his plans to visit the Gambia. I was elated, though part of me doubted that it would happen. Nevertheless, I started counting down the days, growing more thrilled as the date approached.

On the day that George arrived in the Gambia, I awoke with excitement and a case of nerves. I wanted everything to be perfect for our first in-person meeting. After taking a shower, I indulged in my favorite perfume, Clive Christian's Jump Up and Kiss Me. I usually kept my routine simple, but that day was different. I oiled my body and prepared myself meticulously. My sister and my assistant were in the kitchen, so I had them make breakfast. At the same time, I focused on creating an impressive atmosphere. I had recently received a special gift of tea, a beautiful set with leaves instead of tea bags, and I knew George loved tea. I took this opportunity to show him how much I cared.

I chose a stunning black dress, one that was figure hugging, with a daring front split that accentuated my curves. As my housekeepers cleaned the entire property and burned incense, I felt excitement and a determination to be the best version of myself. I wanted to impress George and show him I could be a worthy wife.

He was late in coming over. This was the first of many times this happened, but I always found a reason to justify his tardiness. Out of concern, I texted and called to see if he was okay. Although I did not hear back from him, I was patient, as I figured he probably wanted to spend time with his family since he just landed at home. He kept me waiting for two hours, but everything felt right when he arrived at my home. He was precisely the man I had been waiting for my entire life. We held hands and walked into my house, where the massive amount of food I had prepared for him waited: eggs, bread, croissants, and more. I asked him what he wanted, and I served him.

While he ate, I kept walking back and forth between the dining room and my kitchen, simply because I wanted him to see every inch of my body. He invited me to join him outside, and we drove to see a property he owned that was close to my house. I did not care about the property; I cared about how he made me feel. When we were alone, he kissed me. I had never felt the way he made me feel.

We entered his beautiful two-story home on the Atlantic Ocean and went upstairs to the master bedroom, which had ocean views. He pulled me closer, we looked into each other's eyes, and when he touched my thighs, my body reacted in a way I never knew a woman's body could. It felt so good, and I wanted more. He was hungry for me, and I was hungry for him.

George and I spent nights together, growing closer every day. He often surprised me with unexpected visits, but sometimes I did not hear from him for days. I understood he had family and commitments, so I tried not to overthink it. I did not want to jeopardize losing him.

We decided to keep our relationship private. I was a public figure, and dating was untraditional in the Gambia. But I was excited. I told a friend I was seeing George and how happy he made me. That woman also knew an ex of his, and word got back to George that I had told someone we were dating. He was angry. He said he was worried about my reputation, so I apologized. Once again, I did not want to risk losing him.

Eventually, George felt it was time for me to meet his family. I was anxious, considering I had three kids and he usually dated younger women without children. Dressed in traditional African attire, my sister and I visited his family home. His mother's presence was intimidating, but she seemed welcoming. After meeting his family, I was filled with joy. It was time for George to meet someone significant to me: my father.

George and I went to see him one evening a few days later. My dad liked him instantly. My dad's religious beliefs emphasized the importance of commitment. George and I discussed marriage and our desire to spend the rest of our lives together, which was part of why we introduced each other to our parents. I would never have married George without my dad's blessing. George wasted no time approaching him to ask for my hand in marriage. We had hoped for more time to plan, but fate had other plans, and we set our wedding date for just two days away. My heart knew I wanted George to be mine. I wanted the world to see us together, proud and united. We excitedly started planning the life we would build together. I had yet to learn it would be so short-lived. So embarrassing. So riddled with deceit.

George and I agreed we did not want a grand affair for our wedding celebration; we wanted something meaningful with our loved ones. Our family and friends supported us wholeheartedly, helping with everything from designing the wedding outfits to decorating my home and catering for the guests. Their love and dedication reminded me of just how blessed I was.

Amidst the whirlwind of preparations, the wedding day finally arrived. Early in the morning, my father came to pray for me, and emotions overwhelmed me. This was the day I had chosen to marry the man I loved, free from any pressure or obligation. The presence of my dad as he prayed for our happiness and blessed the marriage meant the world to me.

My hairdresser and makeup artist worked their magic. The traditional religious ceremony was set for 5:00 p.m. at the mosque, and elders from our families would be present. During the ceremony, as I prayed with my prayer beads, the Iman performed the marriage rituals, and the call came. I was officially Mrs. Manneh. My heart burst with joy, and I enjoyed the tradition where the single ladies playfully hit the bride on the head to find their husbands.

However, amidst the happiness, something seemed off about George. He appeared restless, often excusing himself to take phone calls. I brushed it off as congratulatory messages from well-wishers. I was on top of the world, blissfully unaware of the outside world. Later that evening, Haddy called from the United States. When I answered, her voice sounded different— almost tearful. I assumed it was because she knew me better than anyone and understood the significance of this moment for me. I assured her of my joy.

We spent our wedding night at my house, and I was sure anyone could hear my giggling from a mile away. I loved George, everything about him, from his build to how his skin melted under my hands. He made me feel incredible. The night was playful and romantic; every moment was perfect. The next day was different. Not only did my best friend from the United States continue to call me, but my dear friend in the Gambia, Manka, who also serves as my chief of staff/communications director, told me to stay off the Internet. I asked him what was happening, and he downplayed it: He informed me a few rumors were circulating about George, but then he told me to remember everyone was entitled to their past.

I finally managed to call Haddy. She was less protective of me than Manka. Messages were circulating online from girls who claimed George had lied to them about our relationship and did not truly love me. Haddy shared screenshots of these messages with me, and my heart shattered. I was torn between denial and heartache. There was an ongoing online discussion between one of George's exes and my sister-in-law, who claimed George had said he married me only because I had placed a spell on him. Amidst all this, a journalist contacted me about the same rumors. Fortunately, she did not publish any stories about my marriage woes, out of respect for me.

Despite all of this, I was committed to George. I trusted George more than I had ever trusted any person in my life before. There was no way I could have been mistaken about him, since I was an intelligent, insightful woman. Our romance had been fast, but our conversations had been very deep. I was sure I knew him, and I was totally convinced none of the rumors were true. I assured myself George had kept our relationship secret because he wanted to protect me out of respect for my position within my country and my father's role as an Imam. I knew George, and I had married him because we loved each other and no longer wanted to hide that from the world. If I needed further proof, which I did not, I knew anyone who had seen us together had no doubt George loved me. I brushed all the uncertainty away.

Everyone loved George. He became an integral part of my bigger family and community. People at the office, even those who were older than him, called him "Uncle George." In my culture in the Gambia, people see me as a mother figure, and they show respect by bowing and referring to me by my first name.

But allegations of George's infidelity prior to our marriage never stopped. In the few days after what was supposed to be the happiest day of my life, I dealt with one message after the other about George. George allegedly saw and slept with other women the entire time I was falling in love with him. When I approached George about the allegations, he had what seemed like a solid explanation. He said he had broken many girls' hearts when we married, so they would naturally say horrible things about him. I accepted his answer.

We escaped the rumor mill during our honeymoon, and it was beautiful. We explored the most rural parts of the Gambia and visited communities where I had spent years working as an activist. George saw the impact of my work, and we both felt proud. We slept in places that were not the most comfortable, we ate whatever food was available, and we never complained. Despite whatever rumors had surfaced between our wedding and the honeymoon, he made me feel truly loved. We were everything young lovers were supposed to be: playful, joyous, and romantic.

Maybe things would have been better if we stayed in rural Gambia forever. When we returned home, I realized the rumor mill had never stopped. Online, some women whom George had previously dated claimed that he was still in love with them. George reassured me I was the only one. Our families supported us and never mentioned the gossip.

But one day, a childhood friend I considered a sister asked to meet with me. Despite George's objections, I agreed to see her. She revealed to me that she and George were intimate just before our wedding. I did not want to believe her. Why had she not shared this before my wedding? Why had she posted a congratulatory picture of me on my wedding day? Then she showed me photos and videos of them together. It got worse. She was not the only woman George had seen behind my back. She said on my wedding day, George was still in a relationship with multiple women in the Gambia and abroad, many of whom were waiting to set a wedding date with him. I started to imagine how these women had felt when they saw my pictures online and learned that I had married their fiancé.

My childhood friend told me she had spoken to George the night before our wedding. She had reminded him of my status within the Gambia and had urged him to be the husband I deserved and not to embarrass me. George had angrily responded to her, "The same way you guys look up to and love her is how she also idolizes me."

I know that should have been the last straw. I felt so much humiliation. As unbearable as this was, one rumor that had spread across the Gambia hurt more than anything: George had alluded to the idea that I had used voodoo or black magic to get him to marry me. I felt betrayed, not because of his past, but because of his insinuation that he would not have chosen me if he had not been under a magic spell. This was the man who had pursued *me*. I had brushed off the initial message stream that materialized the night and days after our wedding. They were haters, I had told myself. I had married a wonderful man, I was in a powerful position, and jealousy had reared its ugly head. But this revelation was something else.

This was not the love I had thought it would be, but I could not leave this man. I loved him deeply. I also needed to save this marriage for my father's sake. My father had allowed me to marry outside my tribe because he wanted me to be happy. He had gone against everything he believed in and had not told his closest family members I was getting married. To get a divorce right after I got married would hurt him terribly. I would try everything to make this marriage work. And I did.

George never took accountability for his actions. He never reassured me I was his one and only. Instead, he blamed me for listening to my childhood friend. He blamed me for believing her words. Slowly, he erased our pictures from his social media accounts. After just three months of marriage, our conversations turned sour, and he announced he would return to the United Kingdom for a few months to let things settle. I thought I would never see him again. A month after his departure, I returned to the United States to dig into work.

Soon after I arrived, I heard that George wanted a divorce. My heart sank. But talk of a divorce changed things for us. We started talking again, and this reignited the flame. It was as if nothing terrible had ever happened. We were like two kids in love all over again. He had me under his spell, and the next thing I knew, I booked a flight to Scotland to see him. I avoided confrontation as much as possible, so when George told me our marriage did not work because I cared more about others' opinions than I did about him, I agreed and apologized.

After I returned to the United States, we kept talking. Eventually, we decided to go back to the Gambia to rebuild our lives. Neither of our parents knew we were seeing each other again, so we decided to keep it quiet. That did not last long. Our families discovered we were back together, and my father encouraged us to take our commitment more seriously. George and I took a trip to Senegal to enjoy time together. However, his actions made me feel that I was not enough for him. To avoid confrontation, I returned to the United States.

I arrived back in New York and went straight to work. A week later, I was asked to return to the Gambia by my political idol and to consider taking a political leadership role in the next election. I was hesitant because I wanted to work on my marriage. I could not imagine my life without my husband. Yet George urged me to return to the Gambia to discuss my political future, even though I was concerned my involvement in politics would put too much pressure on our marriage. Part of me hoped George would be against my entering politics and would say he just wanted us to enjoy our marriage without any drama or complications. Instead, he told me he was very excited and wanted me to go for it. He promised he would stand by me through it all.

George was my rock for much of the campaign, which I will talk about shortly. Yet the pressure took a toll on him, and our arguments escalated. The day before my thirty-second birthday, he booked a flight and left the Gambia. He walked out of my life without having the courage to tell me. I eventually returned to the United States, and George sent his spiritual guide to inform me he wanted a divorce.

At that point, I would have remained with George, because I was so much in love with him. I had never believed in polygamy, but I would have consented to him having other wives, even though I had seen what sharing her husband had done to my mum. I was open to that possibility and now understood why my mum had stayed with my father. And I had already experienced being a second wife in my last marriage. Yes, I would have been hurt by George having other wives, but I would have accepted it, because I loved him more than I hated polygamy. I would not have been threatened by another wife. By this time in my life, I was more confident in who I was. I was confident in my sexuality and sensuality and would not have been intimidated by another woman. Yes, I would have wanted boundaries. I would not have interacted or lived in the same house with another wife.

This revelation about polygamy made me wonder if I even believed in monogamy anymore. Remember, I grew up in a family and society where polygamy was accepted. And then I fell deeply in love and married a man who cheated on me. It killed me and made me wonder if human beings were meant to be monogamous. I had always wanted to have my husband, my man, somebody I could enjoy life with. Exclusively. But I wondered if it was possible. Were Western beliefs making me look too narrowly at marriage?

Besides my crushing pain, which took a few years to come back from, the rift with Haddy was one of the most painful parts of my relationship with George. Most people can recall a handful of childhood experiences that impacted them deeply. In my case, these experiences often revolved around Haddy. Our history goes back to when we were ten and were both navigating our preteen years in the same neighborhood. An innocent era of shared games, secrets, and promises to be best friends forever.

Haddy was not like any other friend I had; she was special. It may be our shared Sierra Leonean heritage, a bond that made our mothers close. They would converse in their native tongue, leaving us with the echoes of shared tales and traditions. As much as we were allies in our playful mischief, Haddy was also the sanity to my madness. Whenever I was too much to handle, my mother would call Haddy. We would talk, and everything would be right with the world again.

The inevitability of growing up meant facing new adventures and challenges. Haddy moved to the United States a year before I did. The physical distance between Maryland, New York, and Atlanta did little to change our bond. She was there for my high school graduation in New York, a solid presence in the crowd. The births of my children and numerous Muslim holidays saw her journey to be with us. It did not matter to her that the father of my children did not particularly care for her. She was there for me, and that was all that mattered.

As the years passed and I established my organization, traveling became a significant part of my life. Haddy, ever the loyal friend, was by my side. We crossed the world together, especially when my children were babies. Through it all, our bond seemed unbreakable.

However, life has a way of testing the strongest of bonds. After Haddy discovered a troubling connection between George and one of her cousins, she informed me and offered a protective shield, like I did for her countless times. The aftermath was tumultuous. Details were shared, secrets were spilled, and blame was placed. My family's pressure and George's influence on me widened the growing chasm between Haddy and me.

Now, when sadness overwhelms me, I face it without her, yearning for the comfort of the friend I thought would be there forever. The pain of losing such a profound connection is immeasurable.

The choices I made and the consequences that followed have left lasting scars on my relationship with Haddy. Despite the challenges, I hold on to the hope that our friendship will be fully restored one day. Despite our estrangement, the love and care between us never truly vanished. Last year, when Haddy became a mother, I felt compelled to be there, even for a few minutes. Her child was an extension of her and, therefore, an extension of our shared past.

Another source of pain has been my children. George cared deeply about my kids, and they felt the same way about him. Even when we stopped talking, he randomly sent messages about the kids, such as "Tell Khadija and the boys that I said hello." I loved the way George interacted with my children, and I encouraged it. Now that he is gone, we all feel the loss.

During my marriage, I became close to George's family. I have maintained a cherished relationship with George's uncle who resides in the United States and works for the UN. Our bond has remained strong, and he has become a dear friend to me. Our conversations are something I look forward to. George's mother held a special place in my heart as she became a maternal figure for me. I cherished her deeply. Now I find myself yearning for healing and reconciliation for any hurt George's family members might be harboring. I have acknowledged that my reactions during the aftermath of the marriage might have caused them pain, too.

In discovering love for the first time, I found heartbreak. I gave George so much of myself. So much money, energy, and time. I gave him parts of me I never knew I had until we met. For so long, I wondered if I could rebuild the trust he shattered, the love he betrayed, and the heart he broke. Now I know I can. I am human, and humans have a tremendous capacity to heal. Even though I kept a strong face while I was broke apart on the inside, I now understand I cannot save everyone else if I do not set an example by saving myself. And yes, I still believe in love. I just need to take a break from it for a while, because I have a lot of work to do for me, for girls, for women, and for the Gambia.

I have also realized that betrayal has been a recurring theme in my life. From being subjected to infant genital mutilation to being forced into child marriage, I have faced numerous betrayals. Despite all of this, as I reflect on my experiences, I see a woman with positivity and hope. People often ask me how I can remain positive and not become bitter. I believe it is because I have a lot of empathy and tend to rationalize things even when they are wrong. It helps me to find a sense of understanding and to refrain from treating others poorly, regardless of how they have treated me. I have always tried to see the good things in life, even when facing difficulties. Being an activist requires optimism and a belief in the power of change.

Yet my life has been a continuous struggle, with one challenge after another. I have never had true peace and have been searching and hoping for it, but it has always eluded me. Regarding George, despite his hurtful behavior, I cannot help but remember the good person he used to be. It is challenging to understand him fully, as there is a stark contrast between his caring and hurtful sides. As his wife, I loved and desired the good side of him. Still, I also have to face the reality of the hurtful behavior without understanding the reasons behind it.

I crave answers and closure, but sometimes life does not offer them. Even though people referred to George in a negative way after our marriage ended, I still grapple with not having all the answers. It is challenging to let go of a situation when I cannot fully comprehend it. At times, George blames me for how people perceive him now. Despite what others have said, I cannot shake the feeling of needing to understand why things turned out the way they did. A psychologist once told me that sometimes we do not get the answers we seek. As someone who values understanding, I have struggled with accepting that notion. But I realize now that I may never get all the answers, and that is something I have to learn to accept and make peace with.

As I was writing this chapter, the significance of healing became more evident to me. I reflected on our shared spiritual guide, who unfortunately passed away on the day I arrived in the Gambia on my last trip there. His passing was particularly poignant as he served as a mediator between George and me, a vital link that connected us. His absence has made me realize how often we take people and relationships for granted.

I do not want to harbor resentment or anger, nor do I want others to feel that way toward me. I hope for a future where we all find peace, where misunderstandings and hurts, whether intentional or not, are mended. I aspire to alleviate some of the pain I might have inflicted and to foster a space where everyone can find healing and tranquility. I genuinely wish for George and me to liberate ourselves from this cycle of hatred and pain. It would be a tremendous relief for us to be entirely free from it.

My relationship with George, like all my relationships, is complex. I recently had a conversation with him and now realize he, too, went through painful moments. It is not lost on me that when I was in pain, I wanted him to understand and feel my pain so much that I did exactly what my mum had done, something I had hated so much. I talked, cried, and wanted people close to me to understand this man had betrayed me. George is a private person, and this truly hurt him. It impacted him in ways I can never understand. I acknowledge that writing about our relationship in this memoir may cause him pain, yet not talking about this time in my life would be dishonest, and I would not be providing an authentic account of my journey.

I do not know if I would do things differently if life permitted a do-over, but now I understand George more. I think it is hard for anyone to fathom the pressures of politics and being with a woman who is always in the spotlight. I do not know if we communicated well. A lot of the things that happened in my marriage were inexcusable, but I still find myself wondering if there was anything I could have done differently. I will always wish that this marriage had worked and that I did not lose the man I believed to be my soulmate.

My journey of rediscovery continues, and each day of my life in New Jersey brings me a step closer to finding my place in the world. Because it is a place where George and I never lived together, liberation from expectations allows me to embrace my individuality and pursue my passions unapologetically. The same is only partially true of the Gambia. When I returned for the first time since my divorce, I was overwhelmed with grief, even after doing so much work through therapy and writing this memoir. So many places reminded me of George, my first real love. But I know I will heal, and the Gambia truly fills my soul. It is where I am happiest in the world.

I do not know what is in store for me regarding love in the future. I know I will go very slowly, will make the right choice for my children and myself, and will lead not only with my heart but also with my body, mind, and soul. I will act as the whole woman I am becoming.

Chapter 20

Becoming a Whole Woman

IT SEEMS A LITTLE STRANGE THAT as a woman who talks about FGM and rape, I still hesitate to write about sexuality and sensuality. I worry about being judged by my religion. I worry about how my family will see me. I fear any discussion of these matters will be perceived as too "Western." Yet the truth for me is that becoming a human means embracing honesty with fierceness. It means to be a whole person, I need to embrace my sexuality, along with my physical, intellectual, spiritual, altruistic, and emotional qualities.

So, I will start with this: As much pain as my marriage to George gave me, he bestowed a very important gift upon me—to experience what love truly felt like physically as a woman. Our physical passion was deep and fulfilling, fueled by love and a true awakening of my sexuality. It took me sixteen years to get to that place after being a shattered fifteen-year-old girl on a forced-marriage bed.

I know people are curious about the effects on sexuality of being a child bride and experiencing FGM. Let me first tackle child marriage. I know from my own experiences and from talking to hundreds of child brides that very few girls are physically, emotionally, or mentally ready to have sex at a young age, even consensual sex. Forced sex in a forced marriage does not lead to a girl discovering her sexuality and sensuality. It does not enable women to become whole. Sex becomes about power, not satisfaction. Forced marriage is nothing more than rape, and despite the sick fantasies some men have, no girl or woman enjoys rape. It is a violation, degradation, and the ultimate form of violence.

Regarding FGM, I get asked many questions about its relationship to sexual pleasure for a woman. The first question often is, does a woman ever enjoy sex if she has had the procedure? The second question is, can FGM be reversed? I will try to answer both of these questions from my perspective.

First, I never enjoyed sex during my first two marriages. During my first one, it was not sex. It was a nonconsensual act. During my second marriage, I could not feel sensation, because of the damage done to my genitals. While my husband and I had an affectionate relationship until my children were born, all I felt was pain during intercourse. I did not know I should feel pleasure. The word *orgasm* was not in my vocabulary.

My curiosity about orgasms began when I was working at the bank in Atlanta and frequently engaged in conversations with a co-worker named Valerie. Valerie was always keen on discussing facts about female anatomy and sexual experiences, something that was foreign to me since I had never had such experiences myself. My co-workers were not shy about sharing their stories and insisting that women could and should be sexually satisfied. They went into explicit detail about not only why but also how.

I was shy and curious about talking about sex with other women. It was shocking to me how open American women were about these matters, which I considered either too intimate or off-limits. Sexual satisfaction was never talked about among Gambian women. The first time I ever talked about sex was during my underground work in Atlanta, when the immigrant girls we were helping started being impacted by teenage pregnancies. I think having those conversations about sex and contraceptives with the girls was one of the hardest and most embarrassing things I had done up to that point in my life.

The parents and community saw it as my responsibility because a few of "my kids" were getting pregnant. I was sometimes hard on both the girls and the boys, because I had a lot of hopes for them and took it very personally every time someone turned up pregnant.

I would go to their homes and lecture them about how this could impact their future and their education. All the girls were respectful and never got mad or talked back at me. They listened and promised to do better. Today most of them are doing exceptionally well.

My focus then was solely on preventing pregnancy. I never talked with them about sexual satisfaction. That was too "Western." Plus, honestly, I would not have been able to answer any questions, since I had never experienced it myself. Yet I found myself yearning for that experience. Remember, one of my primary love languages is touch, and according to my personality type, I am spontaneous and passionate. It is not surprising I wanted more, but I knew it was not physically possible for me, because of FGM.

In 2017 I underwent FGM reversal, a procedure pioneered by Dr. Pierre Foldès. Essentially, this was a restoration procedure. The operation focused on my clitoris; my labia, which had been damaged during FGM, were not altered. I did not explore options for plastic surgery on my labia since my primary goal was to recover sensation in my clitoris, the most sensitive part of a woman's body. My surgeon removed the scar tissue left in the area where my clitoris used to be and pulled some of the internal clitoris out to reexpose it. The procedure was excruciating and required an entire month of recovery. After the surgery, the recovery of sensation became my primary concern, and I did not dwell too much on other possible modifications. I have found FGM reversal to be very much worth the ordeal.

My ex-husband, whom I left several months after the procedure, might attribute our divorce to the changes that ensued post-surgery, because the restoration equipped me with a newfound understanding of my body. His assumption is wrong. I had been feeling very trapped for years. But I will say that by enabling me to perceive certain sensations, the surgery seemed to restore my confidence.

Not only was my recovery physical, but it was also a journey of rediscovery, as I was encouraged by my doctor to understand my body better through personal exploration. Post-surgery, I began experimenting with toys and focusing on sexual self-satisfaction, and this opened new avenues in my relationship with my body. Quite a discovery at age twenty-eight! Again, from a cultural perspective, this was outside the norm. Self-satisfaction is frowned upon in the Muslim community, although men and women do indulge. They just keep it very private.

It is important to note some women can experience sexual pleasure after FGM and do not need to have a reversal. A number of women I know who have undergone FGM can still feel a range of sensations. Therefore, it is incorrect to assume FGM unequivocally terminates a woman's capacity for sexual satisfaction. However, in my case, as with many other women, FGM robbed me of sexual pleasure. That is why the reversal surgery was important to me.

Also, I want to be very clear that having FGM reversal surgery did not make me promiscuous. An argument often put forth by proponents of FGM is that it is necessary to protect young women from randomly giving in to the pleasures of the flesh. I did not engage in that kind of behavior. With George, I found a fulfilling sexual relationship coupled with love, and this created a beautiful and profound connection between us.

As a women's rights activist, I strongly advise women to embrace their sexuality without guilt, and this entails encouraging them to explore their bodies and to communicate openly with their partners about their preferences and dislikes. It is essential to break away from the societal norm of women suppressing their true feelings, including faking sexual satisfaction to conform to their partners' expectations. It is time to encourage openness and honesty, to foster a culture where women can enjoy their sexuality naturally. At this phase of my life, I am embracing my whole woman era. It signifies my journey toward becoming a complete woman. I am learning to understand and love my body just as it is and to focus on things that bring me joy. That's one reason I talk boldly about this topic in this book, although I know I will receive criticism for my candor.

Sexuality and sensuality are indeed significant facets of my transformation, but they do not solely define my evolution into a whole woman. Becoming a complete woman demands a lot more. It is a process of evolving into a better version of myself, a version grounded in newfound confidence and reflective of the growth I have experienced over the past few years. The support I received from working with L'Oréal has been instrumental in this journey.

In becoming a better version of oneself, one must also actively address other issues that promote a sense of wholeness, or what I think of as health—financial, spiritual, physical, and mental health. One cannot make the journey from victim to survivor to activist to human without integrating all of these. For me, the area that needed my focus was mental well-being.

Chapter 21

A Focus on Mental Health

M ENTAL HEALTH IS A SUBJECT I hold close to my heart, having battled various aspects of it most of my life. Describing this turmoil is not as straightforward as explaining a physical ailment; I have often wished I could exchange it for a more tangible pain, one that people understand better. The anxiety I have experienced often manifests as a heightened heartbeat, shaking, and a whirlpool of incomprehensible thoughts that even I find hard to understand. There have been instances where the anxiety was so overpowering I could not even step out of my home or mingle with others, not because I did not wish to, but because it felt physically and emotionally impossible.

I experienced anxiety as a young girl. The seeds were sown early, then nurtured by the domestic violence I witnessed and the constant upheavals in my life, including the time spent in the United Kingdom when my mum was ill. After she passed away, the pressure on me to get married became a prevalent topic of discussion, even during her funeral. People asserted that marriage was necessary to prevent me from becoming pregnant due to my strong-willed nature. This notion unsettled me terribly, especially given the timing—while I was mourning my mum's death. Essentially, from the moment she died, I felt lost and in need of protection.

Moving to New York so quickly afterward only intensified this anxiety. I was only fifteen when I was forced to marry a man over twenty years older than me. I experienced intense physical pain, caused by FGM and a callous husband who cared nothing about it. I was constantly told the problems were mine alone, and my husband was not wrong in abusing me. I was the bad wife. It was a time of unbearable stress and sadness.

Following the end of my marriage, I lived with my aunt and uncle in New York City but felt a constant unease, unsure if I would have to leave suddenly. Additionally, the instability of being an illegal immigrant and the sexual assault I endured at work heightened my anxiety. I constantly worried about losing my job or being asked to move out. All this happened while I was trying to finish high school in a new school and country. Fear seemed to permeate every aspect of my life. This perpetual fear trained my mind to anticipate the worst at every turn, and so I kept expecting another misfortune to befall me. It was a relentless cumulative cycle of experiencing adverse events and anticipating more. This affected my mental well-being.

I was isolated and trapped in my first and second marriages. I did not want to be there during the first one; and as for the second one, it took me twelve years to mentally extricate myself. With George, the end came as a shock, which made the entire experience even more devastating. The upheaval started the day before my birthday, when he left, promising to return within a few days. However, he never returned, and I was unprepared to deal with it. I had allowed myself to envision a future with George, had opened myself up to feelings I had feared for a long time. His departure significantly affected my mental health, but it was a kind of trauma I had not anticipated. Now I realize I struggle immensely with any loss, be it the death of a loved one or a separation from someone I care about. Loss puts me in a state of significant depression.

Depression brought waves of sadness, loneliness, self-hate, and a constant feeling of unworthiness. It made me question why I could not have the supportive family others seemed to enjoy, and this led to a cycle of self-blame for every unfortunate event in my life. Adding to my ongoing battle with anxiety and depression was a diagnosis of PTSD, which, in hindsight, seems quite obvious, considering the series of traumatic experiences I had gone through.

Here's the irony. I never truly understood the importance of mental health. In the Gambia, the general belief was that people with mental health problems were visibly unstable or "crazy" individuals wandering the streets without any awareness. Discussing feelings like anxiety or sadness was frowned upon, as it indicated a lack of faith in God. I knew I could not share my struggles with my family, because they believed that accepting everything as destiny—including my mother's death—was a testimony of one's faith.

This belief system forced me to keep my fears and anxieties to myself. In terms of my own relationship with God, I fervently prayed and sought God's guidance, especially during times of confusion and despair. My faith has been a source of solace and has helped me navigate through the challenges thrown my way. But it has not been a replacement for the self-care I need to protect my mental well-being.

Mental health issues are common in my family but are rarely addressed. While those of us exposed to Western social media engage in conversations about it, the broader community often attributes mental health issues to black magic or supernatural influences. For instance, when my brother fell ill, he received traditional treatment because it was believed someone had cast a spell on him. I have frequently been told that my attire invites evil spirits into my body, which is perceived as the root of my anxiety.

Being an activist adds another layer of difficulty to protecting myself mentally and emotionally. Relaying my own story repeatedly is a taxing process; it does not bring me comfort. And I find myself immersed in trauma almost daily due to the distressing stories others share with me. People reach out to narrate incidents of death due to FGM, experiences of forced marriage, struggles to escape with children, and feelings of being utterly lost, with no place to turn. These narratives deeply affect me, as they often resonate with my own experiences. Moreover, the inability to assist every individual amplifies my anxiety and depression. This is when I feel a surge of depression and sadness, which frequently manifests as crying. My emotional involvement in my work is profound; as an activist, I feel the pain of others intensely.

I also grew up in a country with a government that killed its own people and jailed them for expressing opposition. People simply disappeared. As I fight for the abolishment of FGM, I understand my efforts can put me in danger. I understand I am a lightning rod for issues regarding women and children. Threats to my life are not uncommon. And as I embark on a more visible political career, there are those who see me as a threat. All this feeds into my anxiety.

Despite the toll it takes, I cannot envision giving up activism, as it is an integral part of who I am. Taking the necessary steps to be safe and protect my family is vital. Equally important, being vigilant about my mental health and seeking necessary help remain crucial. Acknowledging my feelings and discussing them in therapy has brought about significant improvement.

Therapy has allowed me to see things more clearly and accept the nature of people around me, with the understanding I cannot change them. Establishing boundaries is crucial, yet it is a skill I have not mastered. I recognize I need to unlearn many behaviors and adopt healthier habits for my well-being and self-treatment. I am committed to identifying and eliminating the triggers that exacerbate my condition.

My primary defense is to remain vigilant, establish boundaries, and safeguard my well-being. I maintain an open stance toward medication, ready to utilize it to manage my condition. I found that channeling my experiences into writing a memoir was a profound act of taking care of myself. My journey of healing from my relationship with George and all the trauma it brought up truly began when I started writing this book. Most importantly, always remembering why I do what I do helps me get through the difficult times. The reason has always been the same. It started with the birth of my daughter and has never diminished. It started with the children.

Chapter 22

Children as Hope

I N 2017 I PENNED AN ESSAY entitled "A Letter to My Children for the World I Imagine in 2030," which ran in the *Huffington Post*. Those words still ring true.

In 2030, my Khadija, you will not have to conform to any man's rule, you will not be anyone's Play-Doh, and you will not be molded into figures of any man's invention.

Come 2030, my baby girl, I hope you will be asking your mom about how she helped make this era the girl generation: a time when your children are born free.

Just because I went through female genital mutilation, it does not mean it is your or your daughters' destiny.

Because I was forced into a marriage against my own will at 15, it does not mean you will not be able to make your own choices.

Just because my childhood was taken from me does not mean yours will be taken.

Because I spent most of my life being told what to do, what to be and how to act, what to say, and being told what it means to be a woman, does not mean you will suffer the same fate.

Because cancer took my mother away from me does not mean it will steal me away from you.

I took action in order to give you control of your own destiny, but also so your children could exercise the same right.

By 2030 women and girls will feel beautiful, despite society's shallow and insensitive standard of what beauty is.

Education will be a requirement rather than a privilege.

My son will not have to risk his life crossing seas in order to find himself a better future.

My brothers and sisters will have long understood we are one, despite where we are from.

We are all foreigners in someone else's land. Actually, we are all foreigners in this world, since it is our destiny that everyone will die.

By 2030 we will have found a cure for cancer and all other illnesses that threaten our existence.

By 2030 we will not be chanting that "Black lives matter," because by then, we will have fully understood that all lives matter.

Come 2030 we will not displace millions of children because of our love for wars and guns. We will not use guns to kill and wipe out our own species.

My son Muhamed will not have to change his name to Michael to find a job. He will not be afraid to say that he is a Muslim, in fear of being called a terrorist.

The world I imagine for my children is one where they are free, happy, and able to choose, make their own decisions, and not be judged by their skin or faith.

We are one, despite where we are from.[10]

That is the future I want for them. I rely on my knowledge, which has come from being a mother not only to my own children but also to thousands of other children around the world. This is what I know: Children are like blank slates, ready to learn and experience the world. When I see children, it reminds me of the time when I was discovering the world, too. They depend heavily on their caregivers in the beginning, trusting them completely. This trust is the cornerstone of our relationship with them. When it is broken, the consequences are deep. I know that from my own life.

Children's numerous questions show their inherent desire to understand the world around them. It is important to nurture this curiosity, which they have naturally. They are very expressive emotionally, experiencing happiness and sadness intensely. It is easy to get swept up in their raw emotions, which sometimes remind us of feelings we have neglected in ourselves. For many years, I tamped down my emotions by living a dual life. When I became a public figure, I played a role once again. I left my curious nature at home when I was growing up and in my marriages. I protected myself by holding in joy and sadness.

As I said, children are extremely vulnerable and rely completely on their caregivers. But as they grow, they start to develop their own personalities and are always eager to understand the complexities of the world around them. Their raw emotions, whether it is joy over a simple toy or sadness from a minor injury, are intense and often teach us about human connections.

Life can be hard for them, often due to unseen troubles and difficulties. I am not just talking about a lack of food, shelter, health care, and education. Sometimes children find it hard to discover their place in the big world because of the turmoil that surrounds them. But their ability to recover and adapt always amazes me. Spending time with children helps me appreciate the simple joys in life and the purity of true emotions. They give me hope for a brighter future and often make me ponder my own life journey.

Writing about my life has also made me reflect on the impact of my activism on my children. Some experts say that the children of activists may suffer since they did not choose this lifestyle. This concerns me, given my limited choices as a child. However, I try to maintain open and honest communication with my children.

Despite the judgments I face daily, I worry more about the potentially misleading perceptions my children might have of me, especially because of the cultural and spiritual differences in our lifestyle. I hope they will eventually see and understand the real me. I regret the moments I could not be there for them, but I take comfort in giving them my all, in ensuring they know they are deeply loved. While I may never share some of the painful aspects of my journey with them, I hope for understanding and compassion.

Reflecting on what I desire for my children, I definitely do not envision them becoming activists. My earnest wish is for them to carve out paths distinct from mine, to explore avenues other than activism. I have candidly expressed my desire for them to avoid taking on the burdens I have shouldered throughout my life. It boils down to their happiness and freedom. I hope that they will experience a life filled with love and joy, where they are not weighed down by the troubles of the world. I yearn for them to have the liberty to just be, to exist in a space where they are not consumed by the problems of others. To live normal lives.

I foster their dreams through open and honest communication. I encourage them to speak their minds, even if it involves voicing discontent with my actions or decisions. I am keen on nurturing relationships with them that are devoid of force and compulsion, fostering an environment where their voices are heard and valued. My children have taken my openness to possibilities to the next level; they want to do *everything*. For example, my son Muhamed tries out a new passion with intensity almost weekly. Photographer. Clothing designer. Artist. Mechanic. So do my other children. Sometimes I wonder if this is the result of good parenting, but seeing the joy they have for life makes me convinced that I am doing something right. I even find myself a little envious. How I wish I had had these options to explore as a child.

This open communication, however, has its limits when it pertains to my personal life. My children know they are loved dearly by my ex-husband and me, despite the burden of our divorce. I avoid discussing the details of our separation to protect them from feeling caught between us, knowing firsthand the harm this can cause. My children are naturally curious about my relationships and personal affairs, yet I maintain a firm boundary to shield them from becoming entwined in the intricacies of my life. I constantly emphasize my need for privacy, discouraging them from prying too much. Looking ahead to the future, I will introduce them to a potential new partner only when I feel the relationship has reached a point of stability. It is a conscious decision on my part to wait until I am certain about the solidity and the potential longevity of the relationship before bringing my children into the fold.

Most importantly, I want them to understand the future is extraordinary, filled with opportunities not only for themselves but also for the two worlds they are part of—America and Africa. But that future will happen for them only if the next generation makes it happen.

Chapter 23

Africa, My Africa

I WANT TO SHARE WITH YOU some numbers about Africa, my Africa. It contains 65 percent of the world's arable land. Ten percent of the world's internal renewable fresh water. Thirty percent of the world's mineral reserves. Eight percent of the world's natural gas. Twelve percent of the world's oil reserves. Forty percent of the world's gold. Ninety percent of the world's chromium and platinum. Those are the statistics the UN shares when talking about Africa.[11]

By 2050 Africa will be home to nearly 25 percent of the world's population, and its middle class will reach 1.1 billion by 2060. The largest telecommunications revolution in the world is happening on the continent, and it is also home to one of the most dynamic economies in the world. The game of geopolitical chess that is being played in Africa by the United States, Russia, China, and others is intense as opportunities for consumers, labor, and resources appear limitless.

But these are not simply numbers to me. Africa is the land of my heart and of my hope. That hope is epitomized by this quotation from a January 2019 essay for the Brookings Institution by Ameenah Gurib-Fakim, the former president of Mauritius and one of my mentors, and Landry Signé, a senior fellow at Africa Growth Initiative: "While narratives over the past few decades have painted a wide range of views of Africa—as a child in need of development, a rising economic power, an imminent threat, a tinderbox of terrorism, poverty, forced migration, and disease—the truth is, as always, more nuanced. One thing is certain: the transformation Africa has undergone in recent decades has been remarkable. Africa is shaping its own destiny and should be referred to as the 'African opportunity' instead of the 'African threat.'"[12]

My own experience as an activist has shaped my perspectives on how Africa must embrace its own destiny. Specifically, I have spent more than a decade working directly with various players in the development sector. As I have expanded into other areas as a politician, businesswoman, and entrepreneur, I have seen the good and the bad of these efforts. I would like to share some perspectives.

Please understand that I am deeply grateful for being an activist, although I truly wish the issues I fight against did not exist. I would love to resign from my role as an activist if we lived in a world where women and children were cherished and respected. That said, being a public activist has given me many opportunities. I have been able to travel and meet so many incredible people. Sometimes I feel guilty about having been given so much. That is why being critical about aspects of the development sector is quite difficult for me. However, I want to be open and honest. Most importantly, I want to provide feedback that may help shape the efforts of policymakers, nonprofits, and others in a more productive way.

As I travel throughout Africa, it is apparent that we, as Africans, must acknowledge challenges as our own. We must actively address these challenges for the betterment of our continent and align them with our development agendas, with the aim of fostering the best interests of our people. During a recent trip, I had an engaging meeting with representatives from the European Union, where I candidly expressed my concerns that one problem that has been created in Africa is an attitude of entitlement, a persistent chorus of "Give me, give me, give me." This has fostered a changing set of cultural norms that interferes with the crucial attitudinal shift needed to combat practices such as FGM and child marriage.

There is a dangerous sentiment brewing, where communities view abandoning practices like FGM as an opportunity for financial exchange with agencies like the EU or the UN. This sentiment undermines the true essence of these changes, which should be geared toward what is right and beneficial for these communities, not toward a quest for monetary gain. I saw this in Liberia, where I interacted closely with communities and traditional leaders. A persistent narrative I encountered focused on what these communities lack rather than the potential benefits that ending harmful practices like FGM could bring to future generations.

Programs often eradicate these harmful practices with monetary incentives, but what is lacking is a comprehensive, holistic approach. This strategy fosters a reliance on development agencies, which threatens the sustainability of their very programs, as communities may revert to old practices once the financial aid ceases. A more effective approach would emphasize education and economic development, which would encourage communities to foster a genuine desire for change, not one driven by short-term monetary gains.

One reason this happens has to do with how the UN Sustainable Development Goals are set up to promote a silo effect. A more holistic approach is needed, particularly concerning women's rights, gender equality, and the fight against gender-based violence. Women in our communities face multifaceted risks. Our efforts must view individuals in their entirety and address potential challenges they encounter at various life stages. Recognizing the interconnectivity of issues such as child marriage and FGM is vital. Addressing them not as isolated problems but as facets of a more significant issue will facilitate more comprehensive and effective solutions.

For example, women's centers should become safe havens where women can communicate openly and receive integrated education and business opportunities, which in turn will foster their empowerment and contributions to society. Poverty is the fundamental root cause intertwined with various issues we aim to address. Initiatives striving to end practices like FGM often stumble upon the hurdle of economic loss for communities and the individuals previously dependent on them. Therefore, we need solutions that provide alternative income streams for women who previously made their living from practicing FGM on girls.

Equally significant is listening, a strategy I have found to be profoundly transformative. Listening not merely to respond but to comprehend even the unspoken words forms the foundation of effective community engagement. This is vital to the success of any development project. When done with wisdom, listening allows us to perceive unarticulated needs and concerns, and this information enables the crafting of programs with a purpose genuinely aligned with the needs of the communities we serve.

For example, Safe Hands wanted to understand why significantly more boys than girls were going on to college, even though high school graduation rates were good for both genders. If you looked at the problem from the outside, you might think the parents were biased, that they did not care if the girls got further education. But the truth was most of the colleges required the girls to travel alone, which made them vulnerable to harassment and violence. Their parents were protecting them. Instead of focusing on bias, a better solution might be to fund safe transportation for girls to get to school and attain a higher education degree.

Another issue I have is how success is measured. All too often, development programs boast about the number of people they have reached without genuinely considering the impact of their initiatives. In reality, these numbers serve more as decorative statistics in reports rather than true indicators of the changes in the community. I propose a shift in perspective; instead of counting the number of women trained as a metric of success, it would be more meaningful to document how their lives have been transformed due to a program. Tangible results, such as business registrations and increased school attendance among children, would be far more reflective of a program's true impact.

In addition, I have observed a discernible degree of judgment and expectation of gratitude from the African communities being served. A more appropriate approach would be grounded in mutual respect and recognition of the dignity of every individual. No one chooses to be born into poverty or suffering. As such, development organizations must divest themselves of the "white savior" mentality, which implies a level of superiority over those they are helping.

Personally, my early activism career with the United Nations cultivated a sense of indebtedness. Over time, it felt like some people at the UN believed they had crafted my identity, an uncomfortable realization for anyone in my position. While acknowledging this, I also recognize the remarkable work carried out by the UN, particularly in local offices. The organization's sacrifices, commitment, and life-changing initiatives in remote areas worldwide command my utmost respect. I have seen UN employees risk their lives every day to reach people who need urgent help. It moves me deeply, and the world should thank them profoundly.

I do wonder if part of the problem is bias. Racial biases are prevalent globally and restrain the progress of many Black communities. It is essential to acknowledge the bitter truths of history and the current state of affairs to work toward cultivating a future where exploitation and selfish gains no longer dictate the narrative. But I also believe it is incumbent upon Black individuals to maintain a sense of pride and love for themselves, and to refuse to use these obstacles as an excuse for not thriving.

I firmly believe lamenting about the things that were not provided for us or dwelling only in history is not a viable path forward. As Black people, we confront numerous obstacles and limited access to opportunities, jobs, better education, and quality communities. Substantial impediments have been a part of our lived reality, and we must acknowledge them. Nonetheless, these barriers should not serve as excuses. Many Black individuals are thriving, having carved out successful paths for themselves, despite these hindrances.

To truly effect change, communities, as well as individuals, need to respect themselves, and one way is by refraining from viewing aid as a handout and considering it rather as a catalyst for genuine transformation. They must recognize their role in fostering change and building a brighter future for succeeding generations. They need to understand the importance of self-love and pride, and this entails rejecting the notion that they are inherently inferior or are owed something.

In this regard, I envision an Africa where its people lead their battles, driven by a deep love for themselves and their continent. One of the core issues we grapple with, especially in Africa, is insufficient self-love. This deficit has historical roots. For instance, some individuals willingly traded our people for goods, such as alcohol and tobacco. This fact casts a shadow on our present-day identity. And the fact that some of our ancestors did not resist but complied with the slave traders is a reality that remains with us. We were indeed subjugated and utilized for labor, and our resources were exploited ruthlessly. Even today Western companies extract valuable resources from Africa without giving much back to the communities they exploit. It pains me to see only a few people reaping the benefits, at the expense of the many. This kind of greed and exploitation is utterly wrong.

To nurture love and self-respect, I advocate for the greater involvement of local partners in development efforts, alongside international experts and consultants. Encouraging communities to maintain their dignity and actively participate in the change process would promote understanding. For example, in Liberia, where considerable funds have been invested, a stark disparity exists between urban centers and the outskirts. This disparity has been exacerbated by the actions of development agencies and has led to a socioeconomic imbalance that was not initially there.

In addition, I would like us to focus on the widespread government corruption plaguing our continent. Across Africa, police and army checkpoints are commonplace, with officials often resorting to harassment to extract small bribes from citizens. This behavior, although unjust, stems from their desperate circumstances, as many live below the poverty line. Their meager earnings barely suffice to make ends meet, pushing them toward corruption. It might be hard for someone from the West to comprehend this. Still, this reality has engendered a systemic culture of corruption.

Regrettably, corruption is pervasive, not just at roadblocks but extending all the way to the higher levels of government, where nepotism and bribery seem to be the order of the day. Contracts are often awarded to incompetent firms, resulting in shoddy infrastructure. It is not uncommon to find ministers engaged in corrupt practices, without a second thought for the welfare of their citizens. Apparently prioritizing their personal gains over the betterment of society, these individuals allow the exploitation of valuable resources, like minerals, diamonds, and gold, with barely any benefits trickling down to the average citizen.

If I were to take up a political leadership position in the Gambia, I could not afford to be a hypocrite. Upholding the values I have expressed in these pages here would be paramount. It is crucial to remain incorruptible and to secure a decent living not through political exploitation but through independent means. This independence allows one to consistently speak truth to power without fearing reprisals. To be a potent activist, one must maintain one's independence. This is vital. Unless one operates from a significant position of authority, working within the system may not catalyze the necessary changes. Ultimately, the goal is to spearhead transformations at the highest echelons of power, driven by a profound love for our people and an unwavering commitment to truth and justice.

Looking ahead, I hold hope because of the vibrant youth population of Africa. Many of us are fervently passionate about this continent. We are unafraid to hold accountable powerful entities, including the UN, the World Bank, and the International Monetary Fund. If we are given an opportunity to lead and serve our people, a significant change can be achieved. The challenge remains to prevent this new generation from succumbing to corruption, which has plagued us in the past. This requires demonstrating a sustained commitment to self-love, raising our voices against injustice, and practicing moral leadership.

The journey toward meaningful development necessitates mutual respect, genuine understanding, and a holistic approach. By focusing on listening, fostering self-love and pride, and adopting metrics that reflect the impact of development programs, we can forge a future where African communities survive and thrive, grounded in dignity and mutual respect. It is a future we all should embrace. And it cannot be realized without better leadership at the highest levels of government.

Chapter 24

Madam President?

A T AN EARLY AGE, I RECOGNIZED that power lies in the hands of politicians. As a young child, I witnessed the student protests outside my family's home in the Gambia. The students had no power. In the United States I was vulnerable because of the laws against illegal immigrants. I had no power. There were no laws that protected children from FGM or forced marriages. We had no power.

That was true in both my countries—the Gambia and the United States. The difference was the United States was a democracy. When I was a small child in the Gambia, Yahya Jammeh came to power in a military coup and stayed there for about twenty years. He even boasted he would rule "for a billion years if Allah decrees it." That changed as a result of the 2016 presidential election. Adama Barrow garnered 45.5 percent of the total votes, while President Jammeh received 36.6 percent. While the elections were peaceful, the transition was not. President Jammeh refused to step down, despite the threat of military intervention by neighboring states and protests throughout the Gambia. I am proud to say many of the same youth volunteers who had fought so hard against FGM and child marriage took to the streets to ensure democracy came back to the Gambia.

President Barrow ran for a second term and was reelected in the first election in twenty-seven years that did not include former president Jammeh, who had fled the country in early 2017, after refusing to accept defeat. I had a front-row seat to the 2021 election since I was running for vice president, with Halifa Sallah as the presidential candidate. Becoming Halifa's running mate was unexpected, and the lessons I learned on the campaign trail were invaluable.

Our party was the People's Democratic Organisation for Independence and Socialism (PDOIS), and our campaign slogan was "Liberty, dignity, and prosperity." Those three words meant a great deal to me since I had been denied liberty and dignity as a child bride and an FGM victim. I was also acutely aware of how many people in the Gambia—particularly women and children—had been denied a life of prosperity.

Our party holds the distinction of being the oldest in the Gambia's history. Rooted deeply in socialist values, our party fervently advocates providing community education and nurturing a populace that is well informed about their rights and harbors a deep affection for their country. We are united in the belief that the pervasive problem plaguing us as Africans is a diminished sense of self-worth and love for our homeland. We believe fostering a deep-seated love for ourselves and our nation would be a powerful antidote to the ceaseless cycle of corrupt politicians, who are elected, only to pilfer from the impoverished masses.

Our party stands as a beacon of integrity in the Gambian political landscape, renowned as the honest political faction in a sea of corruption. Our leaders have consistently upheld the highest standards of honor and morality, steering clear of any form of corruption throughout their tenure. Their legacy is one of unstinting dedication to serving the populace with utmost integrity, thereby paving the way for a brighter, more prosperous future for all.

My own entry into a political campaign began with a phone call I received from Halifa after I abruptly returned to the United States after another fallout with my husband while we were in Senegal. Halifa is the one political figure in my country whom I held in the highest esteem, as he had always been a beacon of inspiration and guidance for me in my political journey. At that moment, he was battling COVID-19, although he chose not to share the gravity of his condition with me. Instead, he implored me to return to the Gambia. He envisioned a prominent leadership role for me in our country and emphasized my presence on home soil was essential to forge a deep connection with the citizens I aspired to serve better. He firmly believed this critical dialogue could not be relegated to a mere phone conversation, especially considering the election was less than six months away.

I had met Halifa five years earlier, when he played a pivotal role at the end of a twenty-two-year dictatorship that had stifled our nation. He was highly respected due to his courageous actions in 2016. When the former president, Yahya Jammeh, declined to accept the results of the 2016 presidential election, many in and outside the Gambia anticipated that war would break out. Many individuals fled the country, including members of my family. Even Adama Barrow, the president-elect at the time, took refuge in Senegal, just like many other Gambians. Despite the widespread fear, I believed that it was crucial for a politician to stand by the people during such critical times. The populace needed their representatives more in moments of crisis than during election campaigns.

As a mass exodus engulfed the country, Halifa chose to stay, working tirelessly to calm the citizens and negotiate with Jammeh, who held substantial respect for him. Halifa regularly communicated with Gambians through national TV to assuage their fears, cementing his status as a national treasure. With unyielding courage, he traveled the streets, spreading messages of peace to the unsettled populace. His presence became a living emblem of hope in our nation, with many holding him in high regard for his bravery and deep-seated love for our homeland.

Back then, I could describe myself only as an ardent admirer; I was utterly captivated by his eloquence and profound understanding of our laws and constitution. Despite the fact that he was in his early sixties at that time, I found him irresistibly charismatic, a sentiment I often expressed on social media, for which I coined the hashtag #JALIFA to symbolize our rapport. Upon meeting me, he perceived an untapped potential within me, a quality I had yet to recognize in myself. It was only years later that his executive assistant revealed to me that Halifa had seen in me a prospective vice presidential candidate, should he seek the presidency. At that time, still in my late twenties, I could scarcely comprehend why he would envision such a significant role for me.

Back in the United States, I reached out to George to share the substance of the phone conversation with Halifa, because I felt the weight of his words and the urgency of the situation. George suggested we deliberate on this further upon my return to the Gambia. Once there, I arranged a meeting with one of the executives of my political party. The gravity of Halifa's call became more apparent. His assistant brought somber news of Halifa's serious battle with COVID-19.

Despite his own precarious health, he had dispatched his assistant to discuss the party's vision with me. It became clear Halifa and other members of PDOIS were grooming me to possibly become the next leader of our party. Overwhelmed and anxious upon hearing this, I knew I could not forge ahead without George's agreement, especially considering our freshly rekindled relationship. Thus, I sought the counsel of a senior member of our party to engage George in a dialogue. This party member elucidated the party's stance and expressed a fervent desire for me to succeed Halifa.

As a young woman who had emerged from the background I hailed from, I was acutely aware I had already shattered numerous ceilings. I realized the journey ahead would be laden with challenges. To be honest, a part of me fervently wished George would reject the idea and would choose instead a tranquil and uncomplicated start to our marriage. But, contrary to my expectations, he was enthusiastic and encouraged me to seize the opportunity, while promising steadfast support throughout the journey.

We shared the news with his mother, who exhibited a mix of fear and joy. Conversely, my father sternly opposed the idea, apprehensive about the reception I would receive. Despite his fears, George and I nurtured a seed of hope, believing fervently that with the right strategies, victory was within reach. Noteworthy was the fact that a large segment of the Gambian population was below the age of twenty-five, aligning perfectly with my demographic. Furthermore, many women, who were known to vote more than men in the Gambia, resonated with my identity and struggles.

As preparations for my campaign launch were underway, we received heartening news that Halifa was recovering steadily from COVID-19 and regaining his strength. During a comprehensive conversation with George and me, Halifa emphasized his firm belief in my potential to steer our nation toward a brighter future. As a gesture of solidarity and support, he proposed to inaugurate our public campaign in my home village, leaving us with a mere two days for organization and mobilization.

That moment was fraught with anxiety and fear for me, given the conservative nature of our community. While community members had previously tolerated my campaigns against FGM and child marriage, I was unsure if my foray into politics would be received with the same level of acceptance, owing to prevailing beliefs regarding women's roles in leadership, particularly in the context of Islamic traditions.

Despite the uncertainties, we utilized those two days to galvanize the youth and party members for the impending journey. Their support was crucial, as we were unsure of the reception that awaited us. Together, we coordinated the transport of numerous supporters, arranging for fifteen buses and procuring around three thousand T-shirts. Throughout this process, George proved to be an invaluable ally, offering unwavering assistance and encouragement.

Meanwhile, internal discussions were ongoing within our party, and they centered on dissecting my prospective role in the forthcoming election and evaluating my readiness for leadership. Initially, several party executives exhibited skepticism toward my candidacy, primarily due to their unfamiliarity with me on a personal level. This resistance was discomfiting, especially considering my return home had been at Halifa's behest and did not derive from a personal pursuit of power or position.

A day before our departure to Gambissara some friends in the United States worked tirelessly to garner support for me while also crafting my political platform and agenda. They developed a website to ensure we had a consolidated platform, though it was not intended for public viewing at that time. Unfortunately, news of the website's existence leaked to the Gambian media within a few hours, causing considerable irritation among many in our political party, particularly those occupying senior leadership positions. They insisted any announcement should have been withheld until the party's executive meeting, where the flag bearer would be officially introduced.

As the media and others inundated me with calls, seeking clarifications, panic set in. During this time, George and I were en route to meet my cousin, as we were tasked with facilitating the transfer of funds to the village to cover the costs of catering for our anticipated guests. Overwhelmed, I suffered a series of panic attacks in the car. Despite George's best efforts to soothe me, I could not shake the feeling that he could not fully grasp the gravity of the situation.

Upon reaching my cousin's place, I shared the unfolding crisis with her. She inquired why I was succumbing to panic. She reminded me that as a Gambian citizen of legal age, I had every right to vie for the position, and she even suggested the formation of a new political party if necessary. Given her prominent position and extensive network within the Gambia, her support was invaluable and somewhat alleviated my anxiety. After a brief conversation, I handed over the funds to be transferred to our village, ensuring the timely preparation for our guests' reception. It amounted to two thousand dollars, equating to one hundred twenty thousand Gambian dalasi, given the exchange rate at the time. After a careful count, she returned forty thousand dalasi, saying she may have overcharged. Despite her teasing suggestion that she should retain the excess amount, I implored her to understand the financial strain on the campaign, emphasizing the necessity of family support during such times. She acquiesced.

As we prepared to leave her office, a call from Manka, my communications manager, interrupted our departure. He presented a different perspective on the website situation, suggesting it might actually work in our favor by garnering free media coverage, a rarity in the African context, where media presence often necessitated financial incentives. He made a compelling case for retaining the website, a strategy that suddenly seemed sensible and lifted my spirits considerably, bringing a smile to my face for the first time that day.

Unfortunately, this shift in mood did not sit well with George. He voiced his discomfort, believing as my spouse that he should be the primary source of comfort and counsel during stressful moments. Despite my efforts to explain Manka's expertise and long-standing professional relationship with me, George remained unsettled, unable to accept that another man wielded influence over me. To avoid further confrontation and appease him, I offered an apology, promising such a situation would not recur.

On the following day we roused ourselves at 5:00 a.m. to head to our political bureau, eager to transport thousands of T-shirts slated for distribution. We had arranged for a truck to lead the way, ensuring the T-shirts would be disseminated by the time we arrived. Alongside my sister, our driver, and one of the aides from George's residence, we busied ourselves with loading the materials into the car. The dawn hours found even George's mother awake, having remained vigilant throughout the night to supervise the printing of the T-shirts.

George's mother, who had embraced me as her own, extended her affection and blessings in a heartfelt ritual practiced by our elders before loved ones embark on significant journeys. She sprinkled cold water in our wake and offered prayers for our safe and successful journey. In that moment, I experienced a profound sense of maternal love, a feeling that had eluded me in my adult life. As I peered into her anxious eyes, I realized the depth of her concern for our venture. To assuage her fears, I kissed and hugged her, promising a return on the same day, since we had no intention to stay overnight. With her blessings and the ritual water at our backs, we set off in a convoy of three cars, including one from George's family and my own vehicle.

The arrival at our party headquarters was a blend of exhilaration and nerves. As many members were meeting me for the first time, I could feel an array of scrutinizing eyes upon us as George and I, hand in hand, stepped out of the car, along with my sister and my daughter, Khadija. The crowd seemed divided in their reception of me, a newcomer who held a prominent position within the party. While some greeted me warmly, others did not hide their reservations and skepticism.

Despite the mixed reactions, I carried myself with grace, adorned in a white *melhfa*, a traditional Mauritanian garment, which covered my body fully, a modest and comfortable choice, especially under the scorching Gambian sun. This garment, favored not only for its aesthetic appeal but also for the comfort it provided, seemed apt for the long journey ahead from one end of the Gambia to my village at the other extreme. This journey marked my first time touring the Gambia as a politician, not an activist.

The atmosphere was joyous overall, since the event marked the first time many were seeing Halifa since his severe bout with COVID-19. No one had anticipated his recovery. I noticed people preparing breakfast in the back, and as I approached them, they began chanting my name in Wolof, a popular local language. They expressed gratitude not only for my service and for my joining the party but also for the profound affection I had for Halifa.

Most women and youngsters showed kindness toward me that day. Many young people had come expressly because they had heard that I would be there and that we were traveling to our village. This warm reception made me realize the party leadership was beginning to recognize the value I could bring. After conversing with many of the women, I proceeded to the other offices, where I greeted everyone I met. George watched over me, constantly giving me approving nods and smiles, often holding my daughter's hand.

Later, George and I stepped back outside to find more people had gathered, many of them young. Shyly, they approached me to confirm if I was Jaha Dukureh. When they received confirmation, they eagerly asked for photographs, making me feel somewhat like a celebrity, although I sensed this did not sit well with some party members. I indulged most who asked for photos and even joined some in dancing and cheer before I returned to our car. There George and I savored *café Touba*, a coffee beverage that held a special place in our relationship. This ritual of sharing *café Touba* was more than just enjoying a cup of coffee; it was almost a spiritual experience for us, fostering countless moments of joy and bonding.

While waiting in the car for everyone to finish their meal and board their respective buses, George and I enjoyed our spiritual music and even engaged in lighthearted gossip regarding the various glances people directed at me. Our drivers mingled with the crowd. Later they would report back that some long-standing party members harbored reservations about my swift ascendancy within the party, feeling it undermined their years of sacrifice and contribution. I understood their concerns, as I, too, harbored doubts about my rapid rise in the party and wished to understand Halifa's rationale in deeming me fit for leadership.

George remained a pillar of support and joy, infusing laughter and happiness into the atmosphere. Eventually, Halifa appeared, and other party leaders joined us in our vehicle for the next leg of the journey. Accompanied by a caravan of musicians and praise singers, we formed a lively convoy, and the vibrant atmosphere seemed to follow us wherever we went. Our journey continued with brief stops in several villages, where locals recognized Halifa and wished to express their gratitude for his service. Each time, he urged me to accompany him, wanting the villagers to see and know me. Rumors circulated, with many speculating about our relationship, hinting at a marital connection due to my youthful appearance. George took these insinuations in stride, sometimes jokingly clarifying that I was his wife and Halifa's daughter.

As we approached a highway village that marked the gateway to my Gambissara, I coordinated our next steps while adorning George in a beautiful white caftan that accentuated his natural grace. My coordination effort was briefly interrupted by a minor disagreement with George over some old photos he had found on my phone, but I managed to keep the focus on our first significant political event. At that point, we were greeted by numerous individuals eager to meet us and show their support for our campaign. Their enthusiasm was evident, and it warmed my heart to witness neighboring communities coming together to support us. A group of young men on motorcycles, wearing T-shirts bearing images of Halifa and me, took the lead and guided us through streets thronged with people.

The townspeople welcomed us with a display of solidarity and warmth that moved me deeply. Here was a place that had once been critical of my views, quick to ostracize me for opposing their cultural norms, and had labeled me Westernized. Now the people were rallying in support of me, ushering in a new era of acceptance and pride. The sheer number of people and the palpable sense of communal joy indicated a significant shift was occurring in the political landscape. From the elderly to the youngsters, every conceivable relative and acquaintance appeared to be present, filling the streets to the brim, even occupying tall buildings and peering through walls to witness my arrival.

On that day, I realized the value of personal growth. Having gone from being a nobody to potentially someone significant, I seemed to gain an extended family overnight. The village now recalled the kindness of my mother and claimed connections to me of various forms. Regardless of whether they truly believed in my presidential aspirations, the images of the day engraved themselves in my memory.

As we approached the town square, where the meeting was to be held, I opted to walk—instead of adhering to the traditional practice of standing on the car roof—wanting to remain close to the people who had come to welcome us. This decision seemed to resonate well, as thousands gathered, filling every available space, eager to catch a glimpse of me. At the town square, I was ushered to a seat traditionally reserved for dignitaries. Despite my initial reservations, Halifa and other party leaders insisted I take the place of honor. The meeting commenced with prayers and warm welcoming remarks from village elders, who recounted the history of my family and the significant role my ancestors had played in the community.

I commenced my speech by expressing my profound gratitude to the village elders, women, youth, neighboring communities, and even the children who had filled the streets to see me. I acknowledged that achieving such support, given my personal history, seemed unimaginable. I thanked them for their affection and pride, which dispelled the notion I had harbored that they despised me. That day, I saw nothing but love and pride reflected in their faces, a validation that filled me with hope and a renewed sense of purpose.

Following my address, Halifa took to the podium and lavished praise on the warm reception we had received. Despite his numerous visits to Gambisara throughout his political career, he admitted that this welcome surpassed any he had witnessed before. He affirmed his belief in my leadership qualities, a conviction fortified by the testimonies and accolades from my hometown.

He emphasized that my deeds and growth had positioned me as a beacon of hope, not just for Gambisara but also for the entire nation. This sentiment was echoed in the nickname bestowed upon me by our traditional praise singers: "Gambisara Jike," which translates as "Gambisara's Hope." Halifa articulated his vision for my role within the party, hinting at major plans brewing for my political future. However, he stressed the importance of seeking blessings from my hometown before embarking on this new journey.

Initially, the plan had been to visit my home and seek the elders' blessing for my prospective leadership role within the party, a declaration meant to be made within the confines of my home-town. However, during our journey, I had gathered that there were voices within our ranks who were advocating for a council meeting prior to any official announcements. Sitting beside me, George grew increasingly restless, suspecting the party members of attempting to exploit my kindness. Despite his concerns, I maintained faith in their intentions, acknowledging many within the party had not yet fully comprehended my background and aspirations. They wondered why Halifa sought to entrust the legacy of Gambia's oldest political party to a relatively inexperienced individual. Despite George's skepticism, I chose to remain open to their approach and found myself dismissing George's warnings often.

Our meeting in Gambisara was an unprecedented success, and perhaps the most significant milestone in our party's history. Following the speeches, we mingled with the attendees, posing for photographs and engaging in uplifting conversations. The area's parliamentary representatives affiliated with our party also graced the occasion with their presence, adding to the jubilant atmosphere.

Later, we retreated to my grandfather's room for a festive dinner with Halifa and Sedia Jatta, a co-founder of our party. During our trip, Sedia and I had begun fostering a deeper connection, a promising sign for future collaborations. However, our departure from Gambisara was marred by an unfortunate incident. As we prepared to leave, a group of young men approached, demanding money. When I explained my inability to provide them with any, they responded by shattering the rear windshield of my car with stones.

Fearing for our safety, I instructed the driver to accelerate in order to avoid any further confrontations. Our vehicle was pursued by individuals on motorcycles, an act that left me baffled and frightened. Considering Gambisara's status as a stronghold for the ruling party, I could not help but suspect the overwhelmingly positive coverage of our rally had incited these acts of aggression. I feared for the safety of my family in the vehicle and pondered the future of my political journey if such incidents persisted.

Inside the car, shards of glass were scattered over us, intensifying my terror. George grasped my hand tightly. Despite my initial fear, his presence provided a source of strength, solidifying our bond as a couple. When we met up with other party members in the neighboring village, they expressed their sympathies for the incident and noted the frequency of such occurrences during road travel.

George, ever the optimist, managed to lighten the mood with his humor, even amidst the distressing circumstances. As our relationship had matured, his role had evolved into that of confidant and partner, a person privy to my deepest secrets and aspirations. His meticulous approach to situations often balanced my more impulsive tendencies, helping us navigate the complexities of the political landscape together. Acknowledging the sacrifices he had made, including leaving his job in Scotland to support my journey, I felt a deep appreciation for his unwavering commitment.

We utilized a plastic sheet to cover the shattered window temporarily, then resumed our journey, accelerating our pace to reach home safely. We arrived home at around 2:00 a.m. and were welcomed by my mother-in-law, who had vigilantly prayed for our protection throughout the night. Her joyous expression at our safe return filled me with warmth. Exhausted and hungry, we shared a quick meal before retiring to our room. The subsequent morning George and I visited the campaign headquarters, where we were greeted by Halifa and other party members. Witnessing the daily congregation of supporters at our headquarters and their dedication to our collective vision filled me with hope.

Our Gambisara rally emerged as one of the most monumental achievements in our party's history, garnering me immense respect within the ranks. Doubts regarding my participation had transformed into unanimous support, with many now rallying behind "Team Jaha." It seemed the populace had recognized my potential to continue the party's legacy and had aligned with Halifa and Sedia's ambitions for our future.

In the following days, we coordinated with our party executive to initiate a nationwide tour across the Gambia. This tour was meant to introduce us and our vision for the country. Halifa had a different agenda for me specifically. He aimed to establish my political identity among the Gambians. Accompanying me on this caravan tour were my sister Geo and my daughter, Khadija. The intensity of the tour took us by surprise.

I had always been aware of my affection for my husband, but it was during the campaign that I became certain of his reciprocal love for me. Our journey took us from one town to another, and we started our day at seven in the morning and sometimes worked until three or five the next morning. The caravan resembled a vibrant procession with music, and it made stops in every village across the country. We organized small town halls in some villages, while in areas with substantial support, we held rallies. Halifa consistently introduced me as a prominent member of the party leadership and gave me the opportunity to address the crowds first. During the tour, I increasingly used local languages, and my proficiency improved notably, especially in Mandinka.

Political tours were an entirely new experience for me. They were more taxing both physically and emotionally compared to any other experience I had encountered before. There were instances of ageism and sexism at various locations where my authority and identity were questioned. During the tour, we formed a close bond with Sedia, which turned out to be a source of comfort and companionship. Sedia became somewhat of a therapist for us, helping us explore the dynamics of our relationship and our individual roles in it.

The tour was not without its challenges, including resistance from some party members regarding my prominent role in the events. It had become apparent that Halifa was grooming me to be the next leader of the party, and this attracted both support and opposition. The journey across the Gambia was educational, offering us a glimpse into the lives of our citizens, their struggles and dreams. Since I came from a privileged background, this was a wake-up call about the disparities existing in our society, and it strengthened my resolve to work tirelessly toward the betterment of all Gambians.

The grueling schedule meant limited opportunities for meals and rest, adding to the strain of the journey. Despite this, the support from George was unwavering. He was a pillar of strength, encouraging me to persevere even when I considered quitting. The bond we shared became our sanctuary amidst the chaos, offering moments of intimacy and connection. However, our relationship faced tests, too, especially when we were back in the city, with access to the Internet and the accompanying distractions and conflicts it brought.

As the nomination day approached, I found myself under tremendous pressure to secure promotional materials for our party, a move that created financial strain and tension between George and me. Despite these challenges, our bond seemed to deepen during our time away from the city, as we were unified against the adversities we faced. Our relationship, marked by affection and camaraderie, garnered attention and support from the local communities.

During the nomination event, I was seated next to Halifa as he received his nomination. He kept me nearby throughout the occasion. By now, everyone in our party understood I was Halifa's selected vice presidential candidate, should we prevail. However, the wider public often mistook me for his spouse or offspring. Initially, Halifa and I found the confusion amusing, but over time, I found it rather offensive. This persistent misunderstanding underscored the prevalent societal view that women are primarily fit for familial roles rather than leadership roles. This became an inadvertent focal point in our campaign, and it called for systemic change. The nomination event went well, and we garnered substantial support from our party members, placing us among the top four contenders in a pool of over twenty presidential hopefuls.

Following the nomination, my personal life began to unravel. As my birthday approached, the distance between George and me widened, exacerbated by our deteriorating financial situation, largely due to my overly generous spending habits. I believe George grew increasingly resentful, feeling my altruistic nature was eclipsing our shared goal of building a family and attaining stability. Tensions escalated further as the election, which we now anticipated losing, drew nearer. On the eve of my thirty-second birthday, George departed for the United Kingdom without even a farewell, leaving me heartbroken and alone during a critical period in my life.

Meanwhile, I continued my campaign efforts, motivated not by ambition but by a genuine desire to serve my community. However, I felt George's growing discontentment cast a shadow over my efforts. His resistance to my campaign commitments, especially my late-night engagements, evolved into a source of frequent arguments. I believe these conflicts were a pretext for George to extricate himself from our marriage. Despite the emotional toll, I persevered, refusing to engage in the drama he seemed to be seeking. My commitment to the campaign persisted, despite personal anguish.

The subsequent loss in the election, coupled with Halifa's retirement, left a heavy burden on my shoulders. Financially drained and emotionally shattered, I decided to return to the United States. Now I had a taste of politics and knew I would not stay away. As a U.S. citizen, I had the choice to run for a seat in the House of Representatives or the Senate. In my heart, I felt I might have found success in American politics. Yet I made the deliberate choice to refrain. It was not because I lacked ambition or love for my adopted country, but rather because I desired to possibly serve in a different, perhaps less conventional capacity—as the president of the Gambia. Some might question this, not fully grasping the depth of my commitment or how much I believe I can lead the Gambia to prosperity for all. I believe I have the ideas and the passion to make a run for the top office, and hopefully, I will win.

In recent years my energy has been channeled into an initiative that I deem pivotal, not only for its intrinsic value but also as an asset for my presidential campaign. This effort, which is named Regenerative Hubs, centers around agriculture. Agriculture is a passion of mine because I know it can transform lives on our continent. I believe that whether it is about improving food security or lifting women out of poverty, agriculture is one of the only ways we can transform our continent. Regenerative agriculture, specifically, is vital because it prevents land degradation and deforestation. It can improve soil, biodiversity, climate resilience, and water resources while creating a more productive and profitable model for farming.

We are reaching out to venture funds and governments for funding of Regenerative Hubs. What I yearn for are investors who can see the depth of my vision and believe in its potential as much as they believe in me.

I had the privilege of presenting one project from Regenerative Hubs to the Liberian minister of agriculture. The Center for Agriculture and Climate (CAC) has recently been provided its first home by the Liberian Government to create a national regenerative agricultural ecosystem. With its base at the Heritage Center near Monrovia, CAC will educate local farmers on regenerative practices, introduce international regenerative certification systems at a national level, implement soil carbon credit systems to incentivize regenerative practices, and enable funding streams to improve food security through new local processing facilities for regenerative products. Regenerative Hubs will also make this project personal by telling the stories of local regenerative farmers and brands to the world.

My history has been punctuated with episodes of me taking calculated risks for causes that resonate with me deeply. A prime example was my crusade to ban FGM. It was treacherous terrain, considering that the country was under the iron grip of a ruthless dictator implicated in the deaths of thousands. The threats and potential consequences did not deter me. I had a goal, a vision, and my resolve was unwavering. This very spirit is what fuels my aspirations for the agricultural project, given its capacity to be transformative.

I feel my ability to see situations with fresh eyes is what is needed for the Gambia's future. For example, starting Safe Hands for Girls was an embodiment of my personal mission to shield my daughter and countless others from the horrors of FGM. As I navigated the landscape of FGM organizations, I was dismayed by the conspicuous absence of survivor-led initiatives. The existing organizations, while numerous, lacked the deeply personal insights only a survivor can provide. This gap spurred my drive to challenge the stereotype that survivors could be only the faces of campaigns and were ill suited to spearhead movements. This flaw in perception was not restricted to FGM and child marriages but spanned various forms of violence. Meaningful change remained a distant dream until survivors, with their unique insights, took the reins.

I also believe strongly in youth, and they believe in me. Young supporters from my political party have been nothing short of inspiring. They have been industriously crafting branding materials that bear my image, name, and an array of slogans. Among those, "President Khaled" stands out. It is a moniker lovingly bestowed upon me by the young leaders of the Gambia.

As an activist, I have been the vanguard for those who often go unheard. The years I have dedicated to activism have endowed me with an empathy few can rival. As a woman and as an activist, I have felt the collective heartbeat of our people. This bond ensures that the interests of the Gambian people will always shape my presidential decisions. My experiences as an activist have not only broadened my understanding of sociopolitical intricacies but have also solidified my conviction that transformative change requires a seat at the table of decision-making.

This understanding, coupled with the sheer potential embedded in political leadership, is the bedrock of my desire to potentially become the president of the Gambia. Politicians, by design, command immense power. They frame laws, manage national coffers, and set the course for their nations. However, the misapplication of this power, which leads to corruption and systemic disparities, has only augmented my ambition. In the role of president, I perceive an unparalleled chance to wield this power judiciously for the betterment of our people.

My aspirations do not stop at simply rectifying past mistakes. The Gambia, with its natural beauty and rich heritage, is a land I hold dear. I harbor dreams for it, dreams of an inclusive, prosperous, and joyful nation. My interactions with global luminaries, such as Richard Branson, stand as evidence of the global doors that can open for our nation under my leadership. A youthful female president can rejuvenate our international image and breathe fresh life into sectors like tourism.

"Madam President?" some might ask with skepticism. But in those words, I see a future where my relentless activism, deep connections with the people, and unwavering dedication to the Gambia's progress come together. A future where I lead our beloved nation to unparalleled heights. In essence, I present all that I am and all that I have gathered over the years as tools to propel the Gambia forward. My ambition is rooted not in the mere acquisition of power, but in channeling power for the greater good.

This goal may seem unattainable. I do not believe it is. I know where I came from, and I know what I have achieved. As one of the youngest Africans ever to be nominated for the Nobel Peace Prize, I have dedicated my life to public service. As a politician and an activist, I have been a leader in the international development and nonprofit sectors. I have been a lightning rod for major progressive change against FGM and child marriage. As a youth leader, I have been adamant about raising awareness in the Gambia and globally and becoming a leading voice of a new generation of African women, a generation rising up to demand equality for women.

My platform, if I run, will be a platform of change by investing more and more effectively in people. I will ensure access to quality health care for all, which includes providing adequate prenatal health care and combating childhood malnutrition. I will help enact legislation that grants young people the right to a proper education, thereby reinvigorating the economy with a well-trained and robust workforce. I will focus on major renovations in infrastructure and on social safety nets that protect the poor.

When I look back and weigh everything, I am buoyed by the promise of what lies ahead. The right backing can catalyze the change I aim to bring, both for the African communities and for my political journey. I carry the lessons from my past, using them as stepping stones to push forward with the goal of enacting lasting positive transformation in our world.

Chapter 25

Final Reflections

W RITING A MEMOIR, PARTICULARLY at thirty-three, is rewarding but challenging. I am such an evolving person because of my age and experiences, and I am both young and old in spirit. In my pursuit of understanding myself and my emotions, I have learned to embrace my multifaceted identity. I am not just a survivor of hardships; I am also a strong, resilient woman who can create positive change in the world. If I do a sequel in thirty years, who knows what I will share or how I will feel? Maybe I would even call it *I Laugh to the World*. So, I leave you with some final reflections at this time in my life.

I never got the chance to be a typical teenager. At fourteen, I lost my mother. Then I found myself in a foreign country, forced into a marriage with a man I detested. With no guidance, I was expected to uphold my family's honor. All I yearned for was an everyday teenage life: to date, to be happy, to have my mother by my side, and to live without fear.

Despite these challenges, I achieved a lot, to the extent that everyone in my country knows me. That means I cannot make mistakes or live like my peers. While they can enjoy simple pleasures, like going to a restaurant or wearing trendy clothes, I am judged for every action and constantly reminded of my responsibilities. I became a recognized hero, and with that recognition, I grew disillusioned with my hero status.

This disillusionment deepened after my marriage, when I realized the immense public scrutiny my husband and I had faced. My entire marriage and subsequent divorce became a public event due to my status. Alongside the personal pain, I struggled with the unexpected celebrity. Although I never sought fame, I accepted it, because I believed it could further a cause I cared about. However, it became nearly unbearable. This fame also hindered my self-discovery.

Having been controlled by my family and then by societal expectations, I have never had the chance to understand who I truly am. I have been a daughter, a wife, and a young mother, and I have always prioritized others over myself. While I do not regret these roles, they have limited my growth and aspirations. The only time I truly pursued what I wanted was when I fell in love with George, but that relationship nearly destroyed me. But finally, I am becoming clearer about my identity and my future.

I am caught between two worlds. The United States and the Gambia are two lands, two homes. When I am in the Gambia, a part of me yearns for the sanctuary of the United States. When I am enveloped in the comforts of America, solitude is an accessible luxury, something I cherish deeply. But in the Gambia, solitude is an elusive treasure. Just this morning, fifteen unexpected guests appeared at my doorstep. As I emerged from my room, the sight of them left me taken aback. As much as community and shared space can be a beautiful experience, there are moments when the soul cries out for solitude.

Recently, I was talking with my siblings about my mum. They wanted to visit me at my house, but I said I wanted to be alone. They saw this as such a Western concept. They said if my mum had witnessed my behavior, she would have been appalled and never accepted that. It would have made her very angry. They said she would have broken every window and glass in my house if she had come over and I had not got up, because I wanted my own space. "One's own space" is not a Gambian construct at all.

The United States has also provided me with the comfort of genuine relationships. I feel surrounded by those who care for my well-being without a hidden agenda. Sometimes I brace myself in the Gambia for the motives lurking behind familiar faces. The lack of trust stems from past relationships, betrayals, and disappointments. The Gambia's tight-knit nature amplifies every ripple in the fabric of my personal life. If I form a bond with you, the odds are you might be related, somehow, to the many intertwined relationships of my past. Everyone's business becomes communal knowledge, making privacy an even rarer commodity.

This became very clear to me after my marriage to George. The pain of my failed marriage weighs heavily on me. I do not desire reconciliation, but I mourn the loss of what might have been. The societal judgment is palpable. Every whispered conversation and pitying glance carries the unspoken message that it was my fault.

My relationship with George forced me to confront my deep-rooted abandonment issues. It was no longer just about a man walking out of my life; it was about addressing everything else that came with it. There has been a noticeable change in me. Things have improved significantly.

That loss also gifted me resilience. When I felt there was no one to help me up, I found the strength within myself to rise. Writing this book has been therapeutic, offering a fresh perspective and an opportunity to reflect and heal.

The dance between the United States and Africa is delicate and fraught with challenges and joys. But the struggle is real, and it is a dance I continue to navigate daily. Returning to the Gambia, I find a mix of comfort and confrontation. On one side, it is home. The sights and sounds are familiar. But on the flip side, my past efforts, through which I supported so many, are now under scrutiny. Some people I have helped are calling me selfish and even trying to tarnish my image.

To some, I have become the epitome of the Westernized woman— too liberal, too free. Yet, ironically, these same individuals are more than willing to reap the benefits of my Western earnings. The judgment is intense and, in some ways, a universal experience. While the Gambia and other parts of Africa hold their stereotypes about the West, they also see it as a beacon of opportunity.

Being in the Gambia is a roller coaster of emotions. There are moments of sheer joy and others of profound introspection. It is not just the opinions of family that affect me but also those of the virtual world. Online, people from similar backgrounds judge me, branding me as "too Western," a label used both as an insult and a joke.

I am always open to listening to people's problems. Lately, many young individuals have approached me and shared their challenges. Their stories touch me deeply, making me even more committed to serving my people above political ambitions. I have been warned about keeping my distance from certain sections of the community if I harbor political aspirations. Still, the decision is clear: if supporting my people means compromising on political roles, then it is not my path.

What hurts is this label of being "selfish." I remember conversations where people told me about the vulnerabilities of those who give too much of themselves. For instance, they said artists and musicians often wear their hearts on their sleeves. Their openness makes them more susceptible to hurt. This resonates with me deeply. In the Gambia, many perceive me differently. They think I am changing or evolving in a way that is not what they want or expect. This shift in perception is hard to digest, especially from those I have assisted in the past. Yet amid these challenges, some remember and appreciate my genuine intentions. Old friends remind me of why I am on this journey of service. Their steadfast support acts as a much-needed anchor. And regardless of these challenges, I am determined to find a balance. I need to care for my well-being, ensuring I am in the right space mentally and emotionally, so I can continue to serve and support those in need.

I have often questioned my self-worth and the value I bring to others' lives. I wonder if people genuinely appreciate and understand the efforts I put into caring for them. At times, it feels like my kindness is taken for granted, and this realization adds to the weight I carry on my shoulders. My past relationship experiences have kept me guarded and cautious about opening up to new people. I fear being judged or rejected for my past, including for my failed marriages. Finding someone who accepts and embraces me with all my complexities and history seems hard. This fear of vulnerability sometimes prevents me from fully connecting with others, leaving me isolated and longing for genuine human connection.

Since my mother passed, anxiety and depression have been constant shadows looming over me. While I had struggled with anxiety long before George came into the picture, he became an unexpected trigger. The past two years in particular have been marked by heightened anxiety attacks, more so following my divorce with him. Living alone and grappling with the aftermath of our relationship have made this arguably the most challenging period of my life from a mental health perspective.

Then there is the backdrop against which all this unfolded: the global pandemic. It is bizarre to think that amidst the chaos of the pandemic, I jokingly referred to George as my "COVID husband." We met during the pandemic, when I felt isolated from the world. Pre-pandemic, I had been engrossed in international conferences and events with friends from all over the world. But from April 2020 until I met George in December of that year, it felt like life was at a standstill.

The pandemic brought along its share of challenges. My usual sources of income, from speaking engagements and university lectures, dried up. My work with the World Bank, which involved extensive travel, was also affected due to travel restrictions. Since I was a single parent without child support, the financial responsibility weighed heavily on me. Combined with the turmoil of the elections and my personal life, it felt like everything I had been avoiding exploded in front of me.

Then there were the people I was deeply connected to and worried about—the most vulnerable among us, women and children, who bore the brunt of the pandemic. The surge in abuse cases during this time was heart-wrenching. Being a human rights activist at the time was quite a challenge: I knew that atrocities were being committed, but I felt helpless about being able to do anything about it.

However, amidst the chaos, there was a silver lining. Although travel was restricted, I was far from idle. My contract with L'Oréal became my lifeline. I directed every penny from it to support women, such as by launching a safety net program during COVID-19. It involved such things as starting a checking service to hiring community-level workers to ensure the safety of vulnerable women. So my work continued. In retrospect, while I might jest about being "bored" during the pandemic, I was busier than ever.

When it comes to happiness, I have been trying to figure out what truly makes me happy. Reflecting on my past, I remember moments of joy, especially when I started my campaign and impacted rural communities in the Gambia. Those moments brought me immense happiness. But generally, I have not experienced much personal pleasure. I have not had the time to explore what brings me joy outside my children and work.

As I write this book, my life is changing quickly, unexpectedly, and in beautiful ways. One example is my recent attendance at the 2023 United Nations Climate Change Conference, more commonly known as COP28, which was held in Dubai. There I presented on Regenerative Hubs and the Center for Agriculture and Climate. I talked about our efforts to empower women farmers globally through a new system of climate-friendly agriculture, one that brings direct economic benefits to them and their families at the same time that it regenerates Mother Earth. I also shared our plans for international hubs in Zambia, Kenya, Costa Rica, the Bahamas, Sri Lanka, and the Gambia. The response was overwhelmingly positive.

When I left New Jersey to head to Dubai, I had no expectations of how my ideas would be received or who I would connect with. I was excited about seeing my dear friend Bogolo Kenewendo, who is part of the Nala Feminist Collective and is a highly respected global economist. Bogolo has been a blessing in my life, and our friendship has grown extensively since we first met at the African Women Leaders Network.

Even with her intense schedule at COP28, we were able to carve out some time together. Hanging with women like Bogolo means the world to me. Over the past year, I have nurtured strong sisterhoods, especially with Bogolo and Sona Jobarteh in the Gambia. Sona came into my life at a time when I needed to be seen and heard, and our relationship continues to grow, and I am grateful for it. She is a Gambian multi-instrumentalist, singer, and composer and is the first female professional kora player to come from a griot family.

COP28 was an opportunity to meet many different people both socially and professionally. As I have shared, I am an introvert by nature, even though I love people. It is sometimes hard for me to get out of my own way. In Dubai I approached the adventure with openness, even questioning some of my own biases. For example, I have never been attracted to men who are not African. On my second day in Dubai, I met Aiden. I saw him from across the room, and the piercings in his ears immediately caught my attention. I like piercings and don't think I have met anyone in a professional setting that loves them as much as I do. The fact that he had multiple piercings was cool, and I was able to relate to him.

Aiden is part of NEXUS, an organization I recently joined. It is a global community that was founded in 2011 to bridge communities of wealth and social entrepreneurship. With over six thousand members from seventy countries, the organization unites young investors, social entrepreneurs, philanthropists, and allies to catalyze new leadership and accelerate needed political, societal, indigenous, financial, environmental, and equal justice solutions. NEXUS is a unique organization, since many of the members come from wealthy families, and it is the next generation of wealthy people that want to make an impact. Most of the time, I don't feel like I quite belong, but I realize that the organization needs people like me, who understand what impact looks like from the ground up.

Hanging out with Aiden helped open my eyes to a different world. We spent days hanging out and doing things that make us both happy. We went to the desert and traveled to Sri Lanka. I am still trying to figure out what this new friendship is for us, but it shows me that I am finally ready to move on and laugh again. It proved that I still have so much love in my heart and so much laughter.

I know one thing that consistently brings me joy: the ocean. There is something inexplicably magical about being near the beach or in the water. I feel a sense of peace and connectedness when I am by the sea. As a child, I loved climbing trees and hunting birds, but as an adult, the ocean has become my sanctuary. It is as if the water calls to me and draws me in, making me feel like I am in sync with the moon and the tides.

I remember when my sister and I stopped one night by a rocky beach on the shores of the Gambia. She was taken aback by how the moon and the water seemed to merge with me, making me feel like a part of the natural world. I can spend hours sitting by the beach, listening to the waves crash and feeling the breeze on my skin. It is a place where I find solace and a sense of renewal. I often drive to a beach near my house in the Gambia when I am stressed or emotional. Sitting there, I feel like all my worries are washed away, and I emerge as a new person, ready to face the challenges ahead.

The ocean is a constant source of joy and comfort. Its vastness reminds me that there is more to life than just my problems and responsibilities. It is where I can find a sense of freedom and peace, even for a little while. In those moments, I am reminded I am more than just a caretaker for others; I also deserve happiness and self-care.

Setting boundaries with my family has been a journey that requires patience and understanding. I am beginning to recognize I do not need to be available at their every beck and call. I must communicate my needs and limits to my family while reminding myself it is okay to say no. This process of self-discovery and boundary setting is essential for my growth and well-being.

Amidst the struggles, I am still a work in progress, but I am proud of my progress. Acknowledging my need for personal happiness and joy is a significant step in reshaping my life. As a parent, I am determined to raise sons and daughters differently, teaching them the importance of self-care and giving them the understanding that they do not need to sacrifice their happiness for others.

I feel enveloped in a wealth of love and camaraderie with friends who have seamlessly transitioned into becoming family members. For instance, one of my closest companions is someone I affectionately refer to as my "baby sister." She, along with many others in my circle, contributes to a joyful and loving environment that constantly uplifts me. Writing this book and meeting Kathy, who has helped guide me during this process, has also been important. She has turned into a friend, mentor, second mother, and someone I can talk to about everything without being worried about being judged. God has gifted me with so many amazing people that have touched my soul and helped uplift me in ways I cannot express.

My online community is special, and the online connections I have made often mirror a familial bond. Their deep concern for my well-being is evident, especially when my absence from social media sparks worries and prompts them to check in on me, showering me with messages filled with genuine concern. This outpouring of affection and attention truly means a lot to me. It is this blend of relationships, both offline and online, that creates a rich tapestry of love and support in my life.

My relationship with my father is strong and nurturing, yet it is in a state of continuous evolution. There are days when I feel utterly happy and at peace, having come to a place where I fully accept him for who he is. Despite realizing we are not perfect and acknowledging the hurt between us, he remains one of my staunchest cheerleaders. At this point in my life, I am embracing the fact that nothing is perfect and am fostering an environment of acceptance and growth.

I find myself on a path of healing and forgiveness with my mother. I've arrived at a place where I've forgiven myself and her, having grasped a deeper understanding of past actions rooted in ignorance. This healing process has been influenced to a great degree by my own experiences as a mother. Now, as I navigate the intricacies of motherhood, I gain a deeper insight into the ramifications of certain decisions I have made, particularly those about my activism work and the time spent away from home. I hope that my children will exhibit the same level of understanding and compassion toward me, that I will have cultivated a nurturing cycle of empathy that spans generations.

I strive nowadays to find more moments of joy outside my responsibilities, to explore my interests and passions beyond my work. Rediscovering myself as an individual with unique desires and needs is a crucial part of my journey toward happiness and fulfillment. I am committed to self-discovery and growth as I navigate the complexities of my life and relationships. Embracing my flaws, setting boundaries, and seeking happiness beyond my responsibilities will allow me to lead a more balanced and content life.

I look forward to the evolution that awaits me, knowing I am on a path to becoming a more authentic, resilient, and fulfilled version of myself. I am excited about the future and finally ready to move away from fighting and surviving to living my full potential.

Dreams have been my anchor, the compass that has guided my journey through the vast expanse of life's uncertainties. They are not just tales passed down through generations. Still, the very fabric of my identity is intimately entwined with my aspirations, my roots, and the legacy I wish to leave behind. Dreams have seen me through my darkest hours, lighting my path with their unwavering glow.

Dreams hold a special significance in the Gambia, where the night sky is sprinkled with stars. They are our internal constellations, guiding our paths just as the stars guide the traveler. The dreams that took root within me were nourished by stories shared under the moonlit Gambian skies, imparted to me by my mother's soft, weathered hands and her words. She was the beacon of my early life, as she taught me to dream even when faced with life's harshest realities. The narratives she shared were not mere bedtime tales but life lessons. They instilled in me a burning desire to effect change, not just within the confines of our homeland but on a global stage.

My crusade against practices like FGM has been personal, but it is more than just my story. Centuries of cultural beliefs and societal expectations are attached to this narrative. Through the shadows of pain and victimhood, my journey transformed into activism, each step echoing the dreams of countless women and girls silenced by the oppressive claws of tradition. Safe Hands for Girls, my organization, stands as a testament to these dreams. It is a sanctuary where dreams, once shattered, find solace and rejuvenation. Every narrative, every tear, and every voice rekindled represents a dream reawakened.

Throughout my journey, I have been heartened by the unity of dreamers. From fellow activists to survivors, their aspirations harmonize with mine, creating a symphony that advocates for a world free from prejudice and harm, a world teeming with possibilities. Yet dreams are living entities. They grow, change, and adapt. My aspirations have expanded beyond my salvation and now encompass a broader vision for a more equitable world.

My sincere wish is to inspire others to dream fearlessly. Ultimately, the power of dreams and their potential to inspire change are best summarized by the joy I find in my work. The children's laughter, the sheer joy in their eyes, and the weight of responsibility I feel reaffirm my purpose. Where some see a burden, I see a blessing. In these moments, I find the peace that has eluded me for so long, the peace only a life dedicated to a dream can bring.

Notes

1. World Health Organization. "Female Genital Mutilation: Key Facts." WHO.int. https://www.who.int/news-room/fact-sheets/detail/female-genital-mutilation.

2. UNICEF. "Child Marriage: Latest Trends and Statistics." https://www.unicef.org/protection/child-marriage.

3. Tina Turner, "What's Love Got to Do with It," Private Dancer, Capitol Records, 1984.

4. Abou El Fadl, Khaled. Speaking in God's Name: Islamic Law, Authority, and Women. Oxford: Oneworld Publications, 2001.

5. *Jaha's Promise*, directed by Patrick Farrelly and Kate O'Callaghan (Ireland: Underground Films, 2017), DVD.

6. *Jaha's Promise*, directed by Patrick Farrelly and Kate O'Callaghan (Ireland: Underground Films, 2017), DVD.

7. "Eleanor Roosevelt Medal," Eleanor Roosevelt Center at Val-Kill. https://ervk.org/about-medals/eleanor-roosevelt-val-kill-past-medalists/.

8. CineONU Facebook page. https://www.facebook.com/CineONU/videos/324402084822032.

9. https://www.youtube.com/watch?v=FgoPgNb65jc

10. https://www.huffpost.com/entry/a-letter-to-my-children-f_b_7205922

11. https://www.unep.org/regions/africa/our-work-africa#:~:text=The%20continent%20has%2040%20percent,internal%20renewable%20fresh%20water%20source.

12. Ameenah Gurib-Fakim and Landry Signé, "Africa's Rebirth: From 'Dark Continent' to 'African Opportunity'," Brookings Institution Essay (January 2019).

FGM Resources

The following is a list of resources about FGM. This list is neither comprehensive nor curated. Please use it as one source to further your understanding of FGM.

GLOBAL ORGANIZATIONS

1. 28 Too Many, www.fgmcri.org
2. ActionAid, www.actionaid.org
3. AHA Foundation, www.theahafoundation.org
4. Amref Health Africa, www.amref.org
5. Coalition on Violence Against Women (COVAW), www.covaw.or.ke
6. Daughters of Eve Foundation, www.daughtersofeve.online
7. Desert Flower Foundation, www.desertflowerfoundation.org
8. Equality Now, www.equalitynow.org
9. FORWARD (Foundation for Women's Health Research and Development), www.forwarduk.org.uk
10. Global Media Campaign to End FGM, www.globalmediacampaign.org
11. International Center for Research on Women (ICRW), www.icrw.org
12. Maendeleo Ya Wanawake Organization, www.mywokenya.org
13. Orchid Project, www.orchidproject.org
14. Plan International, www.plan-international.org
15. Population Council, www.popcouncil.org
16. Sahiyo, www.sahiyo.org

17. Save the Children, www.savethechildren.net
18. Tahirih Justice Center, www.tahirih.org
19. The Girl Generation, www.thegirlgeneration.org
20. The Guardian Global Media Campaign, www.theguardian.com
21. Tostan, www.tostan.org
22. UNICEF, www.unicef.org
23. World Health Organization (WHO), www.who.int
24. World Vision, www.wvi.org

REGIONAL ORGANIZATIONS

Africa

1. Action Health Incorporated (Nigeria), www.actionhealthinc.org
2. Afrik International (Sierra Leone), www.afrik-international.org
3. Egyptian Initiative for Personal Rights, www.eipr.org
4. Maasai Women Development Organization (Tanzania), www.maasaiwomentanzania.org
5. Women Advocates Research and Documentation Centre (Nigeria), www.wardcnigeria.org

Asia

6. AIDOS (Italian Association for Women in Development, Italy), www.aidos.it
7. Babiker Badri Scientific Association for Women's Studies (Sudan), www.bbsaws.org
8. Cimra Welfare Trust (Pakistan), www.cimra.org.pk
9. Sahiyo (India), www.sahiyo.org
10. Samraksha (India), www.samraksha.org
11. WADI (Iraq/Kurdistan), www.wadi-online.org

Europe

12. Forward UK (United Kingdom), www.forwarduk.org.uk
13. Federation of Somali Associations in the Netherlands (FSAN), www.fsan.nl

14. KWISA (Kenyan Women in Scotland Association, Scotland), www.kwisa.org.uk
15. Mediterranean Institute of Gender Studies (Cyprus), www.medinstgenderstudies.org
16. National FGM Centre (UK), www.nationalfgmcentre.org.uk

North America

17. End FGM Canada Network, www.endfgm.ca
18. Sahiyo US, www.sahiyo.org
19. End FGM/C U.S. Network, www.endfgmnetwork.org
20. There Is No Limit Foundation (USA), www.thereisnolimitfoundation.org
21. Tostan (USA, operating mainly in Africa), www.tostan.org

Oceania

22. Australian Muslim Women's Centre for Human Rights, www.amwchr.org.au

ACTIVISTS

1. Aissatou Sow Sidibé: Activist and politician in Senegal; follow her activities through news media and interviews.
2. Alimatu Dimonekene: Activist and founder of ProjectACE Initiative; follow her on Twitter @TheAlima.
3. Bogaletch Gebre: Late Ethiopian activist who founded KMG Ethiopia; learn more about her legacy at www.kmgethiopia.org
4. Efua Dorkenoo: Late activist known as the "mother" of the global movement to end FGM; her work continues globally through various organizations.
5. Farida Ado: Nigerian author and activist; follow her work through her publications and media appearances.
6. Hibo Wardere: Activist and author; follow her work through her website www.hibowardere.com or on Twitter @HiboWardere.

7. Ifrah Ahmed: Somali Irish activist; follow her work through the Ifrah Foundation at www.ifrahfoundation.org or on Twitter @IfrahFoundation.

8. Jaha Dukureh: Gambian activist and founder of Safe Hands for Girls; follow her work through the website www.safehandsforgirls.org or on Twitter @JahaENDFGM.

9. Khadija Gbla: Australian activist; follow her work through her website www.khadijagbla.com.au or on Twitter @KhadijaGbla.

10. Leyla Hussein: UK-based activist and psychotherapist; follow her through her website www.leylahussein.co.uk or on Twitter @LeylaHussein.

11. Lorna Andisi: Kenyan activist; you can follow her on Twitter @AndisiLorna.

12. Mariya Taher: U.S.-based activist and co-founder of Sahiyo; follow her through the website www.sahiyo.org or on Twitter @mariyataher83.

13. Masooma Ranalvi: Indian activist and founder of WeSpeakOut; follow her work at www.wespeakout.org or on Twitter @RanalviMasooma.

14. Nimco Ali: Somali British activist and co-founder of the Five Foundation; follow her on Twitter @NimkoAli or visit www.thefivefoundation.org

15. Nyaradzayi Gumbonzvanda: Zimbabwean human rights lawyer; follow her on Twitter @vanyaradzayi.

16. Purity Oyie: Kenyan activist; follow her activities through public platforms and interviews.

17. Rugiatu Neneh Turay: Sierra Leonean activist and politician; follow her work through media coverage and interviews.

18. Sarian Karim Kamara: UK-based activist; follow her work through her organization Keep the Drums, Lose the Knife.

19. Soraya Miré: Somali American filmmaker and activist; follow her work through her films and public speaking engagements.
20. Waris Dirie: Somali model, author, actress, and social activist; follow her work through her foundation at www. desertflowerfoundation.org or on Twitter @Waris_Dirie.
21. Yasmin Mumed: Canadian activist; follow her activities through her public speaking engagements and interviews.
22. Zainab Bangura: Sierra Leonean politician and UN representative; follow her work through her public service engagements and UN platforms.
23. Zeinab Eyega: Executive director of Sauti Yetu Center for African Women and Families; follow her work at www. sautiyetu.us
24. Zubaida Bai: Indian engineer and social entrepreneur; follow her work through her website www.zubaidabai. com or on Twitter @zubaidabai.

BOOKS ABOUT FGM

1. *Cut: One Woman's Fight Against FGM in Britain Today* by Hibo Wardere. This autobiography recounts the personal experiences of Hibo Wardere, who underwent FGM as a child in Somalia.
2. *Desert Flower: The Extraordinary Journey of a Desert Nomad* by Waris Dirie. In this autobiographical book, Waris Dirie shares her story of undergoing FGM as a child in Somalia and her subsequent journey to becoming a top fashion model and a UN Special Ambassador fighting against FGM.
3. *Do They Hear You When You Cry* by Fauziya Kassindja and Layli Miller Bashir. This book narrates the true story of Fauziya Kassindja, who fled Togo to escape forced marriage and FGM and sought asylum in the United States.

4. *Female Mutilation: The Truth Behind the Horrifying Global Practice of Female Genital Mutilation* by Hilary Burrage. Hilary Burrage explores the cultural, moral, and societal pressures that sustain FGM.
5. *The Girl with Three Legs: A Memoir* by Soraya Miré. Soraya Miré recounts her personal experience of undergoing FGM in Somalia and explores how it impacted her life. The memoir also discusses her activism against the practice in the United States.
6. *However Long the Night: Molly Melching's Journey to Help Millions of African Women and Girls Triumph* by Aimee Molloy. This book tells the story of Molly Melching, an American woman who has worked for over four decades to educate and empower communities in eight African countries in order to bring about social change, including the abandonment of harmful traditions, such as FGM.
7. *Warrior Marks: Female Genital Mutilation and the Sexual Blinding of Women* by Alice Walker. Alice Walker, the Pulitzer Prize–winning author of *The Color Purple*, explores the origins, justifications, and consequences of FGM, combining personal narratives, testimonials, and analysis to present a comprehensive view of the issue.

MOVIES ON FGM

1. *The Cut: Exploring FGM* (2017). This documentary attempts to unearth the underlying reasons for the continuation of FGM in various communities across the globe. It features interviews with survivors, activists, and community leaders, who discuss the harmful practice.
2. *The Day I Will Never Forget* (2002). This documentary by Kim Longinotto gives a deep insight into the lives of young Kenyan girls who oppose the tradition of FGM in

their communities. The film presents personal narratives and the legal endeavors to shield girls from this dangerous practice.

3. *Desert Flower* (2009). Based on the autobiography of Waris Dirie, this film narrates the life journey of Waris, a Somali model who underwent FGM as a child. She later became a UN Special Ambassador and fought against the practice. The movie explores her trajectory from a childhood in Somalia to success as a model and her activism against FGM.

4. *A Handful of Ash* (2017). This documentary film delves into the practice of FGM in Iraqi Kurdistan, highlighting the persistence of the practice, despite an official ban in place in the region.

5. *In the Name of Your Daughter* (2018). This documentary portrays the courageous stories of young Tanzanian girls who risk everything to escape FGM and child marriage, emphasizing their bravery and resilience.

6. *Jaha's Promise* (2017). This documentary narrates the story of Jaha Dukureh, an activist and FGM survivor, who stands up to the harmful tradition of FGM in her home country, the Gambia.

7. *Moolaadé* (2004). Directed by Ousmane Sembene, this film showcases the story of a woman in a small African village who offers protection to a group of girls seeking refuge from FGM. The film critically examines the conflict between tradition and modernity.

8. *Warriors* (2015). This documentary follows a group of young Maasai warriors in Kenya who reject the practice of FGM and strive to foster change in their communities by advocating for the abandonment of FGM.

Child Marriage Resources

The following is a list of resources about child marriages. This list is neither comprehensive nor curated. Please use it as one source to further your understanding of child marriages.

GLOBAL ORGANIZATIONS

1. ActionAid, www.actionaid.org
2. Breakthrough, www.letsbreakthrough.org
3. CARE International, www.care-international.org
4. Child Helpline International, www.childhelplineinternational.org
5. ECPAT International, www.ecpat.org
6. Equality Now, www.equalitynow.org
7. The Girl Generation, www.thegirlgeneration.org
8. Girls Not Brides, www.girlsnotbrides.org
9. Global Fund for Women, www.globalfundforwomen.org
10. Human Rights Watch, www.hrw.org
11. International Center for Research on Women (ICRW), www.icrw.org
12. International Planned Parenthood Federation, www.ippf.org
13. Oxfam International, www.oxfam.org
14. Plan International, www.plan-international.org
15. The Population Council, www.popcouncil.org
16. Save the Children, www.savethechildren.net
17. Terre des Hommes, www.terredeshommes.org
18. Tostan, www.tostan.org
19. UNICEF, www.unicef.org

20. UN Women, www.unwomen.org
21. Women's Refugee Commission, www. womensrefugeecommission.org
22. World Health Organization (WHO), www.who.int
23. World Vision International, www.wvi.org
24. Young Lives, www.younglives.org.uk
25. Youth For Change, www.youthforchangeglobal.org

REGIONAL ORGANIZATIONS

Africa

1. Agape Family Care (Zimbabwe), www.agapefamilycare. org
2. FORWARD (Africa), www.forwarduk.org.uk
3. MIFUMI (Uganda), www.mifumi.org

Asia

4. ARROW (Asia-Pacific Region), www.arrow.org.my
5. Asha Nepal, www.asha-nepal.org
6. Blue Veins (Pakistan), www.blueveins.org
7. Sahil (Pakistan), www.sahil.org
8. Shakti Samuha (Nepal), www.shaktisamuha.org.np

Europe

9. Astra (Serbia), www.astra.rs
10. ECPAT UK (United Kingdom), www.ecpat.org.uk
11. La Strada International (Europe), www. lastradainternational.org
12. PAPYRUS (UK), www.papyrus-uk.org

North America

13. AHA Foundation (USA), www.theahafoundation.org
14. Canadian Women's Foundation (Canada), www. canadianwomen.org
15. Girls Not Brides USA, www.girlsnotbrides.org/ our-partnership/national-partnerships-coalitions/ united-states/

16. Tahirih Justice Center (USA), www.tahirih.org
17. Unchained At Last (USA), www.unchainedatlast.org

South America

18. Equimundo (Brazil), www.promundoglobal.org
19. Fundación Paniamor (Costa Rica), www.paniamor.org
20. Tamarindo Foundation (El Salvador), www.tamarindofoundation.org
21. THEMIS (Brazil), www.themis.org.br
22. Wara (Bolivia), www.wara.org.bo

ACTIVISTS

1. Agnes Pareyio: Prominent Kenyan activist. Follow her activities through public platforms and news.
2. Dr. Faith Mwangi-Powell: Renowned activist, former global director for The Girl Generation, and CEO of Girls Not Brides. She is active on various public platforms.
3. Graça Machel: Prominent activist focusing on children's rights. She is widely covered in the media and has official platforms.
4. Jasvinder Sanghera: UK-based activist and the founder of Karma Nirvana, a specialist charity for victims of honor-based abuse and forced marriage in the UK. Follow her work on Twitter (@Jas_Sanghera_KN) and other platforms.
5. Kakenya Ntaiya: Kenyan educator and activist. Follow her work through her foundation's website: www.kakenyasdream.org
6. Lakshmi Sundaram: Former global executive director of Girls Not Brides. She has been vocal about her stand against child marriage. Follow her work on platforms like Twitter (@lakshmiunwomen).
7. Malala Yousafzai: Well-known activist focusing on education for girls. She has a significant presence in the media and on platforms such as Twitter (@Malala).

8. Memory Banda: Malawian activist who has been fighting against child marriage. Follow her activities through her official public platforms and interviews.

9. Nankali Maksud: Senior adviser at UNICEF who is actively involved in initiatives against child marriages. She often shares her views on public platforms.

10. Payal Jangid: Young activist from India who has been a vocal critic of child marriage. You can find out more about her through her public appearances and media coverage.

11. Rachel Lloyd: Founder of Girls Educational & Mentoring Services (GEMS), an organization that fights against sexual exploitation and child marriage. Follow her work through the organization's website: www.gems-girls.org.

12. Sonita Alizadeh: Afghan rapper and activist who uses her music to fight against child marriage. Follow her work on platforms like Twitter (@SonitaAlizadeh).

BOOKS ABOUT CHILD MARRIAGE

1. *Before We Were Strangers* by Renée Carlino. While not focusing exclusively on child marriage, this novel delves into the repercussions of early marriages and how they can impact individuals' lives.

2. *Child Bride: The Untold Story of Priscilla Beaulieu Presley* by Suzanne Finstad. This biography recounts the life of Priscilla Beaulieu Presley, who was married at a very young age to the famous singer Elvis Presley.

3. *I Am Nujood, Age 10 and Divorced* by Nujood Ali and Delphine Minoui. This is a memoir of Nujood Ali, a Yemeni girl who made international headlines when she obtained a divorce at the age of ten and freed herself from an abusive marriage.

4. *Nujood Ali and the Fight Against Child Marriage* by Katherine Don. This book portrays the broader scenario of child marriage through the lens of Nujood Ali's courageous journey.

5. *The Pearl That Broke Its Shell* by Nadia Hashimi. This novel tells the interweaving stories of two Afghan women, showcasing their struggles and resilience. Child marriage is a major theme throughout the book.

6. *Sold* by Patricia McCormick. A powerful narrative that portrays the harrowing experiences of a young girl sold into marriage. This book provides insights into the grim world of child trafficking and forced marriages.

7. *A Thousand Splendid Suns* by Khaled Hosseini. This novel, chronicling the lives of two generations of women in Afghanistan, touches upon the theme of child marriage as one of the characters is married off at a young age.

8. *When Dreams Travel* by Githa Hariharan. This fictional narrative weaves in the theme of child marriage as it tells the stories of two women in different timelines, offering a poignant commentary on the lives of women through the centuries.

MOVIES ABOUT CHILD MARRIAGE

1. *The Day I Will Never Forget* (2002). This feature documentary by Kim Longinotto examines the practice of female genital mutilation as it recounts the experiences of various Kenyan women and girls who courageously take a stand against the practice.

2. *Difret* (2014). Based on real events, this Ethiopian film portrays a precedent-setting legal case in which a young girl is kidnapped for marriage and kills her abductor, setting off a chain of legal and social repercussions.

3. *I Am Nojoom, Age 10 and Divorced* (2014). This Yemeni drama narrates the true story of Nujood Ali, a Yemeni girl who fought for her rights and set a legal precedent by obtaining a divorce at the age of ten in order to free herself from an abusive arranged marriage.

4. *Lakshmi* (2014). This Indian drama, which explores the issues of child trafficking and forced marriage, follows the story of a fourteen-year-old girl who ends up in a child marriage and fights against the odds for justice.

5. *The Man Who Knew Infinity* (2015). Though it is not centrally focused on child marriage, this biographical film about famous mathematician Srinivasa Ramanujan hints at the issue, as Ramanujan was in a marriage arranged at a young age.

6. *Moolaadé* (2004). Though primarily focused on the subject of female genital mutilation, this Senegalese film also touches on the topic of child marriage, showcasing the practice in a small African village and one woman's fight against it.

7. *The Pear Tree* (1998). This Iranian film delves into the themes of childhood and innocence by portraying an older man who reminisces about his childhood love and an arranged engagement that occurred during his youth.

8. *Wadjda* (2012). An inspiring Saudi Arabian–German film that, in addition to telling the story of a girl who aspires to own a bicycle in a conservative society, sheds light on the nuances of child marriage in Saudi society.

9. *Water* (2005). Set in 1938, this Canadian film, written and directed by Deepa Mehta, explores the lives of widows at an ashram in Varanasi, India. It delves into various social issues, including child marriage, as one of the central characters is a child widow.

Economic Empowerment/ Development Resources

The following is a list of resources about economic empowerment and development. This list is neither comprehensive nor curated. Please use it as one source to further your understanding.

INTERNATIONAL ORGANIZATIONS

1. Accion International
   - Website: https://www.accion.org/
   - A global nonprofit dedicated to creating a financially inclusive world, with a pioneering legacy in microfinance and fintech impact.
2. African Development Bank (AfDB)
   - Website: https://www.afdb.org/
   - A regional multilateral development financial institution established to contribute to the economic development and social progress of African countries.
3. Asian Development Bank (ADB)
   - Website: https://www.adb.org/
   - A regional development bank established to facilitate economic development in Asian countries.
4. Bill and Melinda Gates Foundation
   - Website: https://www.gatesfoundation.org/
   - A private foundation that works to help all people, particularly those in developing countries, lead healthy, productive lives.

5. BRAC
   - Website: https://www.brac.net/
   - A development organization dedicated to alleviating poverty by empowering the poor to bring about change in their own lives.
6. CARE International
   - Website: https://www.care-international.org/
   - A major humanitarian agency that fights global poverty and provides disaster relief.
7. Center for Global Development (CGD)
   - Website: https://www.cgdev.org/
   - A think tank that conducts research on and analysis of international development policy.
8. Chemonics International
   - Website: https://www.chemonics.com/
   - An international development company that promotes meaningful change in developing nations.
9. Development Alternatives Incorporated (DAI)
   - Website: https://www.dai.com/
   - A global development company working on the front lines of international development, tackling fundamental social and economic development problems.
10. Economic Commission for Latin America and the Caribbean (ECLAC)
    - Website: https://www.cepal.org/en
    - A UN regional commission to encourage economic relationships between Latin American and Caribbean countries.

11. Enterprise Development Centre (EDC)
    - Website: http://www.edc.edu.ng/
    - A Nigerian institution that provides knowledge, support services, and entrepreneur-optimized infrastructure to enhance business growth and competitiveness.

12. Food and Agriculture Organization of the United Nations (FAO)
    - Website: https://www.fao.org/
    - A specialized agency of the UN that leads international efforts to defeat hunger and improve nutrition and food security.

13. Grameen Foundation
    - Website: https://grameenfoundation.org/
    - An organization that enables the poor, especially women, to create a world without poverty and hunger.

14. Heifer International
    - Website: https://www.heifer.org/
    - A global nonprofit working to eradicate poverty and hunger through sustainable, values-based holistic community development.

15. Inter-American Development Bank (IDB)
    - Website: https://www.iadb.org/
    - The largest source of development financing for Latin America and the Caribbean, with the goal of achieving economic and social development in the region.

16. International Finance Corporation (IFC)
    - Website: https://www.ifc.org/
    - A member of the World Bank Group, offering investment, advisory, and asset-management services to encourage private-sector development in less developed countries.

17. International Labour Organization (ILO)
    - Website: https://www.ilo.org/
    - A UN agency that sets international labor standards and promotes social protection and work opportunities for all.
18. Mercy Corps
    - Website: https://www.mercycorps.org/
    - A global team of humanitarians who partner with communities, corporations, and governments to transform lives around the world.
19. Oxfam International
    - Website: https://www.oxfam.org/
    - A global movement of people working together to alleviate poverty and injustice.
20. TechnoServe
    - Website: https://www.technoserve.org/
    - A nonprofit organization that provides business solutions to poverty in the developing world.
21. United Nations Development Programme (UNDP)
    - Website: https://www.undp.org/
    - The UN's global development network, advocating for change and connecting countries to knowledge, experience, and resources to help people build a better life.
22. United Nations Industrial Development Organization (UNIDO)
    - Website: https://www.unido.org/
    - A specialized agency of the UN that promotes industrial development for poverty reduction, inclusive globalization, and environmental sustainability.

23. Women's World Banking
    - Website: https://www.womensworldbanking.org/
    - A nonprofit organization that focuses on giving more low-income women access to the financial tools and resources required to achieve security and prosperity.
24. World Bank
    - Website: https://www.worldbank.org/
    - An international financial institution that provides loans and grants to the governments of low- and middle-income countries for the purpose of pursuing capital projects.
25. World Trade Organization (WTO)
    - Website: https://www.wto.org/
    - An intergovernmental organization that regulates international trade to ensure that trade flows as smoothly, predictably, and freely as possible.

REGIONAL AND LOCAL ORGANIZATIONS

1. Aga Khan Development Network (AKDN)
    - Website: https://www.the.akdn/en/home
    - A network that includes development agencies focusing on various sectors, such as health, education, and economic development, and working globally.
2. Agence Française de Développement (AFD)
    - Website: https://www.afd.fr/fr
    - A French public development bank that facilitates projects to improve daily life in developing and emerging countries and in French overseas territories.
3. Asia-Pacific Economic Cooperation (APEC)
    - Website: https://www.apec.org/

- A regional economic forum fostering the growth and integration of the Asia-Pacific region.
4. Association of Southeast Asian Nations (ASEAN)
   - Website: https://asean.org/
   - A regional organization that facilitates economic, political, security, military, educational, and sociocultural integration among its members and other Asian states.
5. Centre for the Development of Enterprise (CDE)
   - Website: https://www.cde.org.za/
   - A joint institution supporting private sector development in African, Caribbean, and Pacific countries.
6. Development Bank of Latin America and the Caribbean (CAF)
   - Website: https://www.caf.com/
   - A development bank fostering regional integration and sustainable development in Latin American and Caribbean countries.
7. Eastern Caribbean Central Bank (ECCB)
   - Website: ECCB
   - A monetary authority that is responsible for monetary policy and financial stability in several Caribbean nations.
8. Enterprise Estonia (EAS)
   - Website: EAS
   - An institution that promotes business and economic development in Estonia and is committed to providing support for entrepreneurship.
9. Ghana Enterprise Agency (GEA)
   - Website: GEA
   - A national agency in Ghana that promotes the growth and development of small- and medium-scale enterprises.

10. Greater Amman Municipality, Economic Development
    - Website: Greater Amman Municipality
    - An agency fostering economic development in the Amman region of Jordan.
11. Greater Mekong Subregion (GMS)
    - Website: GMS
    - Program promoting economic cooperation among the six Southeast Asian countries that comprise the Greater Mekong subregion.
12. Invest India
    - Website: Invest India
    - A national agency facilitating investment in India by serving as the first point of reference for investors.
13. Kenya Vision 2030
    - Website: Kenya Vision 2030
    - A development program with a blueprint that aims to transform Kenya into a middle-income country offering a high quality of life to its citizens by 2030.
14. Pacific Community (SPC)
    - Website: SPC
    - An international development organization that promotes, through science, knowledge, and innovation, sustainable development in twenty Pacific island countries and territories around the Pacific.
15. Pacific Islands Forum (PIF)
    - Website: PIF
    - An intergovernmental organization fostering cooperation between the countries and territories of Oceania.

16. Pacific Tourism Organisation (SPTO)
    - Website: SPTO
    - An intergovernmental organization promoting the sustainable development of tourism in the Pacific region.
17. Small Enterprise Development Agency (South Africa, SEDA)
    - Website: SEDA
    - A South African agency offering business development and support services for small enterprises and cooperatives.
18. Trade and Development Bank (TDB) - Eastern and Southern Africa
    - Website: TDB
    - A bank that supports economic and trade development in eastern and southern African countries.
19. West African Economic and Monetary Union (WAEMU)
    - Website: WAEMU
    - An organization of eight West African states that fosters economic integration and development in the region.
20. Western Cape Economic Development Partnership (South Africa, WCEDP)
    - Website: WCEDP
    - A collaborative organization promoting economic growth in the Western Cape region of South Africa.
21. Zambia Development Agency (ZDA)
    - Website: ZDA
    - An agency fostering economic growth and development in Zambia through trade, investment promotion, and business development.

22. Zimbabwe Economic Development Agency (ZIDA)
    - Website: ZIDA
    - An agency facilitating investments in Zimbabwe to foster economic development.
23. Zurich Economic Development
    - Website: Zurich Economic Development
    - An organization that promotes the economic development of the Zurich region in Switzerland.

Acknowledgments

I HAVE TALKED ABOUT THE MANY PEOPLe in this book who have been part of my journey. I have named some, but I am sure others have been inadvertently left out. You know who you are, and I sincerely thank you.

I Scream to the World has been a long and intense effort by a small group. I have been assisted by Kathy Palokoff, chief igniter at goFirestarter, a company dedicated to helping changemakers become authors. She lent her talents and book-writing expertise pro bono so that my resources could be channeled into Safe Hands for Girls and other efforts I am involved in. A huge thank-you goes to her.

Kathy also engaged her three sons in what she describes as "the project of my heart." Matt's insights were particularly valuable since he is a former Peace Corps volunteer in Guinea and is currently chief of the party on a significant project in Cambodia to preserve biodiversity, conserve natural resources, and enhance community livelihood—all causes close to my heart. I send my thanks to the Edwardsen crew.

Kensington Publishing, an independent, family-owned book publisher, has believed in this book from the beginning. I have been honored to work with Leticia Gomez, editorial director of Kensington's Dafina Books imprint, which focuses on race and cultural identity. Working with Leticia has been a joy. And a special thanks to the fabulous copyeditor, Rosemary Silva.

Zeynep Sen, my literary agent from WordLink, brought the book to Kensington. She has constantly supported my work and is a highly talented advocate for all her authors. This book would not have happened without her.

Finally, and most importantly, I want to thank my three children and my team at Safe Hands for Girls and Regenerative Hubs. Writing a memoir is intensely time consuming and emotional. Their unconditional support allowed me the space to make it happen. They have been and will always remain what sustains my soul.

Epilogue

On July 15, 2024, the Gambia's lawmakers rejected a bill that would have overturned the 2015 ban on FGM. The rejection of this proposed legislation was a vital victory for women and girls. If the final bill had been passed, the Gambia would have become the first country to overturn a ban on the practice.

Just five months earlier, the pro-FGM bill had been introduced by a National Assembly lawmaker and then approved by a majority of the members of Parliament. Their argument was that the ban violated citizens' rights to practice their culture and religion. The proposed bill needed three readings for final approval. At that time, many people believed the repeal was a done deal because of the powerful forces at work.

While highly disturbed that the anti-FGM legislation was under attack, I knew that feeling hopeless would only bring victory to those who did not understand the profound effect of FGM on women, girls, and the world as a whole. All the activities I was involved in—both professional and personal—came to a halt. We had a crisis on our hands. I moved back to the Gambia where I joined others, using my voice and influence to be highly visible to our supporters and detractors. I helped activate global support for our cause. I had done it before; I could do it one more time. Once again I was a prominent face for abolishing FGM, although I had wanted to move on to focusing on economic equality for women and finishing this memoir.

We fought tirelessly against the bill, uniting grassroots organizations, connecting with influential like-minded individuals, and mobilizing our communities. We took our message to politicians, sharing personal stories and statistics to paint a vivid picture of the consequences of FGM. We argued that rescinding the ban would harm the health of women and girls, violate their rights, and was a cultural practice, not a religious mandate. Navigating the complex world of politics, using social media effectively, and organizing large-scale events were invaluable in winning this victory.

Many nights were sleepless, filled with relentless campaigning, and the toll was significant. My physical and mental health suffered, and there were moments of extreme exhaustion and despair. There were—and continue to be—death threats as I was vilified by many. But the support and courage of the women and girls working so hard to keep this ban in place kept me going.

When the lawmakers voted against the new legislation, it sparked joy and relief. We had stood on the right side of history once more, showing that even if they burn down our country, we will rebuild to protect our women and girls. Throughout the fight, I learned even more about the power of grassroots movements and the importance of community. I was surrounded by incredible people—from dedicated activists and supportive politicians to influencers and everyday citizens. Working with such a diverse and passionate group reaffirmed my belief in the power of collective action.

I also relearned an important lesson. It is never truly over. Even as we make strides and celebrate victories, the need for vigilance is constant. There will always be new challenges, but I am ready to continue this journey, knowing I am not alone. Together, we will persist, ensuring that the rights and bodies of women and girls are protected now and always. This is a lifelong commitment, and I am honored to be part of it.

To my daughter Khadija and all the young girls who inspire me daily, this fight is for you. Remember that your voice matters; together, we can create a future where every girl is safe, valued, and free. We need to keep screaming to the world.